"My Heart is a Raging Volcano of Love for You!"

Awakening to At-One-Ment Volume II: Liturgical Explorations Collects, Blessings, Litanies, Prayers & Eucharistic Prayers

Kevin G. Thew Forrester

Copyright © Kevin G. Thew Forrester 2011

All rights reserved.
No part of this publication may be reproduced, stored in a retrieval system or transmitted in any form or by any means, electronic, mechanical, photocopying, recording or otherwise, without the prior permission of the publisher.

Published by
LeaderResources, LLC
PO Box 302, Leeds, MA 01053
800-941-2218   <>   www.LeaderResources.org

Cover art © Dianne Mcfadden | Dreamstime.com
Back cover and end page photos © by Marlys Murray

ISBN
978-1-59518-055-1
1-59518-055-9

Contents

Acknowledgments 5
Foreword by Donald Schell 7
Foreword by Louis Weil 11
Introduction 17

Collects
Year A 35
Year B 73
Year C 103

Litany, Prayers, Prayers of the People, Blessings
Litany of Healing 133
Prayers 134
    May We
    A New Heart
    Beholding a Messiah
    Who is a God like You
    Freedom Prayer
    Serene Light
    May We Rejoice
    Welcome Jesus
    Tonight You Reveal
    God of Hope and Promise
    Holocaust Prayer: Create in Us Clean Hearts, O God
    Ash Wednesday: A Way Through the Wilderness
Prayers of the People 141
    Form: Loving Spirit
    Form: We are Grateful
    Form: Litany for Baptismal Ministry
Blessings 146
    Forever Loving, Beautiful, and Good
    Christ, Our Own Heart

THE GREAT THREE DAYS
Maundy Thursday: Sent to Serve 147
Good Friday: The Cycle of Suffering Ceases 149
The Easter Vigil: Celebration of Life Renewed 154

WELCOMING AND SENDING FORTH MEMBERS
Liturgy for St. Paul's, Marquette, MI 155

BAPTISMAL COVENANT
Liturgy 157
  Gathering
  The Presentation for Baptism
  The Renewal of Baptismal Vows
  Prayers of the People
  Thanksgiving Over the Water
  The Baptism

EUCHARISTIC PRAYERS
The Abiding Word 165
Celebration of Creation 168
Nativity 171
Swimming in the Sea of Joy 173

ENDNOTES 177
BIBLIOGRAPHY 179
ABOUT THE AUTHOR 192

ACKNOWLEDGEMENTS

> Every child has known God,
> Not the God of names,
> Not the God of don'ts,
> Not the God who ever does
> Anything weird,
> But the God who knows only 4 words
> And keeps repeating them, saying:
> "Come Dance with Me."
> Come Dance.[i]
> *Hafiz*

In the mid-1990's I had the great fortune of being welcomed as the vicar of the Native American Community, Church of the Four Winds, in Portland, Oregon. Our worship experience in many ways planted the seeds of my practical inquiry into liturgical inculturation. If liturgy is an invitation from the Beloved to join the dance of gratefulness, what would the movement of this community look like? God wants to dance with us – specific people, living at a particular time and in a certain space, inheritors of a rich history. How are we to come and dance with God? Thank you, Tim Brown, Ramona Soto-Rank, Chris Smith, and Anne Scissons, for extending your hands to me, as we learned our sacred dance.

As a ministry developer in the Diocese of Eastern Oregon, Bishop Rustin Kimsey encouraged me to seek counsel from Louis Weil of the Church Divinity School of the Pacific, as St. Alban's Church in Redmond sought to develop a healing liturgy reflecting our baptismal vision of life and ministry. Once again I was learning how to dance. The steps had changed, as had the lyrics and the tunes, but divine invitation was the same: "Come Dance with Me."

For the past ten years I have lived and worked in the Diocese of Northern Michigan, where I am forever grateful for the encouragement of Jim Kelsey, our late bishop, whose unwavering support of exploring creative liturgical expression meaningful to those of us sojourning in the 21st century, enabled me and the community of St. Paul's, to continue to learn the divine dance of love. The Episcopal Ministry Support Team has also been a faithful partner as I have endeavored to integrate the work of early fathers and mothers, as well as the mystics, while in dialogue with Buddhism, Judaism and Islam, to find new liturgical expressions with ancient roots.

For the past 4 years I have gathered each month with the members of the Marquette Interfaith Forum. Together we learn, through conversation, study and wonder, about our diverse sacred paths. Rodney Clark, Nancy Irish, Paul Lemberg, Mohey Mowafy and Aaron Scholnik: I am honored to travel with these friends. As we gather in circle, Baha'i, Unitarian, Soto Buddhist, Muslim, and Jew, I discover anew what it means to dance as a follower of the way of Christ.

My soul continues to be formed by the Narrative Tradition of the Enneagram. I could never have dreamed that within this wisdom school would lie the invitation to rediscover the early church and the mystics. Here, too, I was introduced to the practice of zazen, finding my way eventually to Ryumonji Zen Monastery, Shoken Winecoff Roshi and Tesshin Paul Lehmberg – Buddhist teachers willing to receive a searching Christian and teach him how to sit and receive. And most especially and dearly I bow with open hands and heart to my teachers and companions in the Diamond Work: how beautiful is the realization that we are simply windows unto the Divine. Even more, we *are* the dance, the very movement of God across the face of creation.

My heart smiles with gratitude for my friends of St. Paul's. Together we grow and are wondrously surprised by where the tides of the Beloved carry us.

I thank Linda L. Grenz, Publisher and CEO of LeaderResources, who has made the publication of this volume possible.

Tom and Brenda Ray, Fredrica Harris Thompsett, Rïse Thew Forrester, and especially Donald Schell, have been and remain indispensible dialogue partners. Their insights and suggestions continually invite me to see anew and grow. Beyond the prison of do's and don'ts; beyond the fear of right and wrong; there is the beautiful Christic ocean of gracious movement freely unfolding. Come dance.

Kevin G. Thew Forrester

FOREWORD BY DONALD SCHELL

As I read Kevin Thew Forrester's new book of liturgical prayers, the flow of words and images moved me from thinking about the prayers, making notes on themes and ideas, and somehow engaging a process of theological reflection "as if we were praying them in church" (and I do laugh at myself for writing this) to simply praying the prayers. It was more than a joy and pleasure to discover this unexpected experience. That these prayers demanded to be prayed rather than just read tells us something crucial about how Kevin approaches the work of crafting prayer for a community. This is not a book of private devotions. The prayers are big enough for many to pray them together. The prayers in this book are theologically rich, but they're no pedagogical or didactic systemization of a doctrinal system. These are prayers for praying, a book of common prayer, of prayers to be prayed in community.

So as I read and prayed through these new prayers, I often sensed how it will be to pray them aloud in and for a community. Each collect, blessing, litany, and Eucharistic prayer will reveal its real value as a congregation prays through the book week by week. The book is a generous, open contribution to the renewal of our church's liturgy. These *are* liturgical prayer and liturgical prayer lives (and is tested) as a people pray it together again and again. Will this happen? Happily yes, though some in our Episcopal church will ask, "*Should* it happen? Who authorized these prayers?"

I believe this book is additionally important to us because it represents a serious answer to the question of whether our teachers and communities should be making new prayers. Many who worked together to write the 1979 Book of Common Prayer said afterwards that it might be our last Prayer Book, that Common Prayer would take on a richer, more diverse meaning as local use and enculturation reshaped our understanding of how prayer makes our diverse communities one. But we seem to be asking this question again in the 21st Century.

As one who knows the phenomenal power of shared prayer and the need for local and authentic adaptation to shape our prayer, I appreciate Kevin's acknowledgment that these prayers were born from a liturgical imagination grounded in a praying community. This book is a joyful, loving affirmation of the presence of the Spirit in the church's life. It's an implicit declaration of what we really mean by "tradition" when the church's tradition lives -

- as the Gospels show Jesus re-imagining familiar, received ritual at the Last Supper,

- as the 2nd Century Didache acknowledges (after offering its Eucharistic prayer) 'let the prophets offer Eucharist (give thanks) as they will,'

- as we have seen tradition grow, correct itself, and make new discoveries in the work of the 18th century Scottish Non-Jurors (whose work outside official channels was decisive in the making of the first American Prayer Book and shaped practice of invoking the Holy Spirit in a more ancient way than most Anglican Prayer books ever since),

- as we've experienced with new liturgy from Taize in France, the Iona Community, and American use of the New Zealand Prayer Book.

These instances and the many, many more that Christian history could offer us, witness to an ongoing process of discovery and to the deeper unity that holds us together. If the church's actual unity in common prayer has never been achieved by strict conformity to established norms, how do we engage a process of discovery like this?

What makes these prayers or any unofficial prayers trustworthy enough to try in community?

One answer to that question is two thousand years old – we learn to trust and discern authentic images drawn from Scripture and Tradition and human experience; we trust living openly in the presence of Christ; we trust and discern the Spirit. These acts of trust (and not meticulous textual and ritual conformity) are what have united Christians from the beginning, so this book roots itself in a tradition of renewal that is both ancient and alive.

But how shall our prayers be contemporary? How do we speak to particular culture and particular time? Missionaries in unfamiliar cultures have asked that question again and again. The collapse of agreed on Christian consensus in our culture including the disappearance of an acknowledged 'mainstream' of Christian thought and practice demands that communities, pastors, and evangelists act like those missionaries again today. How shall our prayers be contemporary? What is the living voice of the Spirit today? With new questions and an ever-shifting culture, what does it mean to be twenty-first century Christian community and with what voice shall we speak?

Like a good missionary, Kevin listens openly and compassionately to the questions and affirmations that he hears around us (broadly, in church community and beyond). The Spirit truly blows where she will. Those outside our community and those least formed in our ways of speaking – at least sometimes - seem to speak questions and affirmations that open undreamt of possibilities, yet possibilities that something deep in us acknowledges as true possibilities, legitimate, godly prodding. What does Jesus say to us, when he commends the Roman Centurion (Matthew 8:10) saying, "I have not found faith like this even in Israel"?

Second, like a good teacher, Kevin believes the old may illuminate or free the new in unexpected ways. 'Tradition' in some people's hands means simply, 'whatever feels familiar – what our grandparents seemed to think was right.' But in a time when many are repulsed at received, conventional Christian teachings, particularly teachings about God's justice and a divine wrath that must be appeased, and teachings that imply an autonomy of humankind that authorizes us to lord it over nature (and perhaps over one another), ancient witnesses – the Odes of Solomon, Irenaeus, the early Eastern Church, the Desert Fathers and Mothers, Syrian Christian poets and theologians, and what has come down to us of Celtic Christianity challenge us to speak a language
    - of blessing,
    - of gratitude for our created humanity
    - of seeing and welcoming our mutual co-inherence in Christ,
and these ancient sources nourish as fresh understanding of what 'Christ all-in-all' means for us, for our sisters and brothers, and for Spirit's wild blessing of truth and freedom.

Two other thoughts –

I'm particularly grateful for this book's follow-through on the three-year cycle of the lectionary. It feels like a piece of unfinished work in our official sources. Compared to what we once had in the 1928 Book of Common Prayer, the 1979 Book of Common Prayer's collects can sound extraneous to the day's readings, more seasonally generic than we hope the rest of the liturgy would be. The International Consultation on English Texts in the Liturgy addressed this problem with *Opening Prayers, Scripture, Related Collects for Years A, B, & C from the Sacramentary the ICEL Collects*. I'm grateful for ten years experience of using this book regularly in church, particularly grateful with solidly thematic collects that we used the Collect of the Day to conclude the Prayers of the People so we could hear the collect's connection to readings, sermon, and prayers. Kevin's new book accomplishes the same goals as well or better.

From my own experience of learning to pray the Eucharistic Prayer in Spanish, I learned to read new texts aloud ahead of any praying them as presider. Particularly with a Eucharistic Prayer, we need to give ourselves over to the prayer, to let it find its own sound and cadences and to feel the particular logic and vision of the prayer if we're going to offer it in our own leader's voice for all to pray with us. Without this attention to praying the new words, we hear reading, perhaps even reading well, but public offering of public prayer truly lives when the leader is ready to pray new words she or he has already begun to make familiar.

So thinking about tradition, new questions, and ancient sources brings us back to appreciating how well Kevin offers us new and deeply traditional prayers, not private or individual prayers, but a legitimate, holy offering of common prayer to be tested in the week to week praying of liturgical communities, real congregations.

I feel privileged to write this preface and bless Kevin's offer of this book to its next and evident unfolding, your community's using it, living with and in it, praying it, as the discernment and noticing happens (for any ongoing community) of where the words we offer are filled with the Spirit's breath.

The Rev. Donald Schell,
President All Saints Company and
founder (with Rick Fabian and Ellen Schell) of
St. Gregory of Nyssa Episcopal Church, San Francisco

Foreword by Louis Weil

When the revision of the American Book of Common Prayer of 1928 was first undertaken, the process envisioned was similar to that of earlier editions of the prayer book not only in the United States, but in general throughout the Anglican Communion. The Standing Liturgical Commission began what it called a 'review of the 1928 BCP' that extended more than a decade, from 1950—1963. During that period, a series of Prayer Book Studies were produced which dealt with the customary contents of the various Anglican prayer books. The purpose of these books was for study and reflection; they were not authorized for trial use.

In general, the changes proposed in these studies were modest in nature, often little more than adjustments of a familiar text. In the first series of these studies (nos. 1—16), the use of Elizabethan English was preserved. To a significant degree, these studies depended upon the contributions of liturgical scholars of the Episcopal Church for whom the seminal work of Archbishop Thomas Cranmer in the sixteenth century remained a powerful influence. When the process of revision was undertaken, the general expectation in the church in the 1950s and '60s was that the process would lead to minimal changes in the 1928 rites. This is evident when one surveys the contents of the first series of studies.

Significant change began in 1967 with the publication of Prayer Book Study 17, a revision of the Eucharistic rite called *The Liturgy of the Lord's Supper*. It marked an initial move to the use of contemporary language, and perhaps most significantly, it was authorized for trial use: the people of God in our parishes and missions were being asked not merely to read through a proposed rite, but actually to pray it.

When the current BCP was authorized at the General Convention of 1979, it was thus the product of a long changing model of the revision process. With this final authorization, it was presumed by many laity and clergy that with the process now complete, the Episcopal Church would enter again upon a long period of prayer book stability. As things turned out, nothing could be further from what actually happened. There were a number of significant factors at play both within the life of the Episcopal Church and in the larger context of Christianity in general. Two major factors were the liturgical movement and the ecumenical movement.

The first of these had already been an influence, although quite minimal, upon the earlier BCP of 1928. But the unfolding of the liturgical movement alongside the ecumenical movement led to the situating of Anglican liturgical revision into the larger context of what was also going on in other churches, most notably for us in the Roman Church and in the Lutheran Church, with which in both cases we shared important aspects of liturgical and sacramental practice. In this regard, it is important to note the opening of the Second Vatican Council and that the first document issued by the Roman Catholic bishops was the *Constitution on the Liturgy,* a document that had significant impact upon the Episcopal Church as well as other non-Roman liturgical churches.

Within the life of the Episcopal Church there were also new pastoral imperatives that required further liturgical development. Among these were enculturation in a tradition which had for four centuries been characterized by its English foundation; the full incorporation of children in the sacramental life of the church, including the reception of Communion from the time of baptism; the full inclusion of women in all levels of leadership in the church, both lay and ordained; and more recently the preparation of rituals of marriage for same-sex couples.

Such imperatives as these required that the church move into what we might call "a larger room." At the pastoral level, in our parish churches, this meant that new pastoral priorities would arise for which the clergy could not simply open the prayer book and find the needed rite. This was (and still is) a new thing in the ministries of ordained leaders. It requires more than merely the opening of the prayer book, but rather that the clergy receive the kind of liturgical formation which enables them to develop new rites, drawing upon the rich resources of the tradition, but rites which fully engage the human reality of the local community.

This ability does not come automatically with ordination. Although some are more gifted in this regard than others, there are basic skills which can be learned and which should be fundamental in the preparation of candidates for ordination. Liturgical leadership now requires much more than merely knowing the rubrics.

It is against this background that I see the importance of the work which Kevin Thew Forrester has done in recent years and which is embodied in this volume. The rites have been tested in use: they have been prayed. And they reflect not only the richness of the tradition which precedes them, but also offer to worshiping communities today fresh images which draw from a wide range of spiritualities. They invite us to move into a larger room, and yet not reject the heritage in which many of us have been formed and which we continue to value. They are a sign to us that a new liturgical creativity is open to us if we will accept both the discipline and the risk to venture forth.

The Rev. Dr. Louis Weil,
James F. Hodges and Harold and
Rita Haynes Professor Emeritus of Liturgics
Church Divinity School of the Pacific

DEDICATED TO:

The community of St. Paul's:
lex amandi, lex vivendi

&

My friends in the work for the Pearl.

HOLY SOURCE
HOLY WORD
HOLY BREATH

Introduction

One of the greatest gifts for me of this brief life is being a papa for my two children and the time we share together in reading and prayers each evening. We talk about our day and sometimes, as the lights dim, yes seem to spontaneously pop open in fear. Anxiety is ours from conception and we develop fear so early: a thunderstorm, a nightmare, a shadow on the wall. The signs of fear are universal: we stop breathing and our mind freezes. We retreat from the threatening world, huddle under the covers, and hope that God might intervene for the best.

A challenge before us as Christians is that we live in a time of much cultural change and fear. The predominant mythic-literal ways of understanding ourselves, God, and church are in transition. It is true that as created beings, change and evolution are part and parcel to our life as creatures of God's creation. And yet, it is also true that the break of the 21st century seems to have ushered us into a teeming flow of accelerated changes. As the church in worship of God, engaged in baptismal ministry, we cannot help but be affected by the cultural whirlwind. However, perhaps we may perceive within the shifting winds a divine invitation to revitalize and reform our tradition.

Liturgy and ministry are of a single whole. The liturgical life of the church is the deep well from which ministry draws its divine vitality, for from the well flows the grace to freely serve. Otherwise baptismal ministry quickly devolves to egoic attempts to *save* the *lost* world.

The eucharistic liturgy of baptism especially celebrates the Living Font from which flows our Trinitarian call as Christians to seek and serve Christ in all persons, to love our neighbors as ourselves, to strive for justice and peace among all people, and to respect the dignity of every human being – divine invitations of life that flow from the one Holy Source.

Meaningful and authentic baptismal ministry cannot take place apart from liturgical renewal. The images of God and Christ and church and world and self inexorably shape our sense of dignity, our notion of justice, and our image of neighbor. How we celebrate in our worship greatly determines how we serve. To paraphrase ancient wisdom – *lex orandi, lex vivendi*. This pithy affirmation points out that the church has traditionally recognized that worship and life are inextricably connected, one reinforcing the other; for better or worse. This book explores new forms of prayer and liturgy that draw upon our ancient catholic tradition in dialogue with our contemporary, post-modern, cultural context. These prayers reflect what I describe as an integral sacramental experience and vision of life, which invite us beyond both the individualism of modernity and the fragmentation of post-modernity.

We need to realize that the liturgy at its heart is a shout, a song, a whisper, a plea, a thanksgiving, of love. We long to be united with the Beloved who ceaselessly gives us birth and calls us home. We cast about for words that might begin to express the cry of our soul to receive the divine kiss whose moisture gives us life.

> Throw away
> All your begging bowls at God's door;
>
> For I have heard the Beloved
> prefers sweet threatening shouts,
>
> Something in the order of:
>
> 'Hey, Beloved,
> My heart is a raging volcano
> Of love for you!
>
> You better start kissing me –
> Or Else!'[ii]
>
> *Hafiz*

We need to be reminded and learn to know directly that the divine kiss is as close as our very breath. The Beloved, who is good and loving and beautiful, breathes over clay and brings creation into being. With each loving breath the Holy Source sustains and carries us. As we surrender, like Christ, and let our soul rest in the Beloved, the freeze on our mind melts, our heart expands, and the shadows become angels.

The Holy Breath is sustaining and carrying us. And there are many angels to discover upon our walls; angels that may point the way to a reformed and revitalized liturgy flowing from the truth of At-One-ment. The Incarnation is one such angel, revealing to us our union with creation and God. The ancient mystery of the Trinity once again recaptures attention, teaching us that our basic stance as human beings is one of grateful receptivity to the Holy Source from which flows all life. The symbolic language of "satan" has the possibility to reveal to us anew the meaning of reconciliation in the face of the blinding force of ignorance, greed, and anger in our lives; dualistic forces that would create the illusion of the "separate other" who is our enemy to be dominated and killed.

INCARNATION

Meister Eckhart saw everyone as the sacred word of God, in whom and as whom Christ lives. This vision of a thoroughly blessed creation led him to understand the reason for the Incarnation in a new way:

> People think God has only become a human being there – in his historical incarnation – but that is not so; for God is here – in this very place – just as much incarnate as in a human being long ago. And this is why he has become a human being: that he might give birth to you as his only begotten Son, and as no less.[iii]

Far from being a magical incursion of the Sacred into the secular; far from being Divine exception to the mundane and natural order; the mystery of the Incarnation, once freed from the shackles of a mythic-literal understanding, reveals a much more profound and comprehensive truth. You. Me. Everyone and every creature we meet. Each and every one is, for Eckhart, an only begotten child of God. Eckhart was asking the church to see all of creation as having life only insofar as it is in God. Apart from God there is only death. Everything, without exception, is the living presence, or incarnation, of God. In the words of Catherine Keller the implication is this:

Incarnation is coextensive with the body of the creation.[iv]

The Incarnation reveals that life as such is incarnation, which is why we have the early patristic refrain, "God became human so that *we* might become god."[v] The Holy Word Incarnate thus becomes a way of perceiving the radical and universal character of God's Presence: each word is holy. We become capable of recognizing along with Marguerite Porete that "all things are consonant with God," and as a result we "find God in all things."[vi]

This new way of understanding the Incarnational nature of baptismal ministry carries the church way beyond the simplistic shores of a passing "system's fix" or an au current "program for revitalization." We are rediscovering the Holy Source from which all life and ministry flows. The tradition of the early Christian fathers and mothers, the Eastern Church, and the mystics, such as Meister Eckhart, Julian of Norwich, and Nicolas Cusa, point the way to recovery and beyond. Here is what some of them have to say about the meaning of the Incarnation:

- ❖ ST. EPHREM THE SYRIAN says of Jesus, "He gave us divinity, we gave him humanity." And again: "Our body was Your clothing, Your Spirit was our Robe."[vii]

- ❖ ST. IRENAEUS declares: "the Word of God, Jesus Christ our Lord, who, because of his superabundant love, made himself what we are in order to make of us what he is."[viii]

- ❖ ST. ATHANASIUS quite famously sings: "God became human so that we might become god."[ix]

- ❖ GREGORY OF NAZIANZUS resounds the refrain: "God is made Man; man is rendered god."[x]

- ❖ GREGORY OF NYSSA teaches us that "Because our nature is mixed with the divine nature, our nature is made divine."[xi]

- ❖ Centuries later, MEISTER ECKHART will remind the church that every single person is called to the mystical life, which is nothing other than the journey whereby we discover we are blessed from the beginning by being one with God. This blessing makes our divinization in Christ possible. To follow the way of Christ is to break through the shadowy fog in order to know from our own experience that "God's ground is my ground, and my ground is God's ground."[xii]

- ❖ JULIAN OF NORWICH sings out clearly that "all will be well."[xiii]

- ❖ NICHOLAS OF CUSA links humanity's deification with the image of the Logos: "I consider filiation of God to be reckoned as nothing else than deification, which, in Greek is also called *theosis*."[xiv]

Within this mystic heritage of tradition we behold a cross, which reveals the boundless depth and breadth of the Beloved's eternal love and forgiveness, rather than being the *cause* to convince God to love and forgive us. Here we move beyond the limited, mythic-literal liturgical confines of St. Anselm, who argued that Jesus was sent by God to be crucified in order to satisfy a debt humanity could not pay. Somewhat ironically, here in the more ancient Eastern Church, we find Christians affirming that the Incarnation is the very reason for creation – so that the Beloved might graciously share the divine life with us. We live in a gracious moment where it is possible to transcend the bounds of St. Anselm's honor-based violent atonement theology.

When we realize that "Incarnation is coextensive with the body of the creation," it becomes much more possible for us to develop what I describe as "an integral sacramental vision": All creation is a sensual symbol embodying and signifying the Beloved's saving Presence. The Incarnation testifies to the sacred character of the womb of life, which is the living font from which flows the gracious capacity for our own healing transfiguration in Christ.

TRINITY: ONE COMMUNITY

I find it quite exciting that within the interfaith dialogue among Buddhist and Christian monks, the symbolism of Trinity has emerged as a focus of conversation. Once again, if we can be released from the grip of the predominant mythic-literal understandings of Trinity, we may discover that life itself is Trinitarian – a grateful dance of gracious love, from beginning to end. (Brother David Steindl-Rast speaks eloquently of our call to lives of Trinitarian gratefulness. See http://www.gratefulness.org/)

Instead of an obstacle to interfaith exploration, the mystery of the Trinity speaks to the universal truth that we receive life from the Holy Source and we gratefully return all we are into the Source. All is *kenosis*, because all is a complete emptying of the heart, mind and body into God. The dance of creation is a dance within the heart of God, in whom and as whom we live and move and have being. Every move is Spirit-inspired and Sprit-borne; there is no other possibility. Christ is the paradigm of the dance, revealing love empty of egoic desire. One God. One Dance. One Community overflowing with gratefulness.

Human life as the image of God embodies the Trinitarian dance of evolution. Two marvelous examples of distinct, yet complementary, visions of our Trinitarian dance are those of St. Ephrem the Syrian and Rublev. For St. Ephrem, says Kilian McDonnell,

> The Sun corresponds to the Father, the light to the Son, and the heat to the Spirit: 'Behold the image! Son and Father, light and sun, the Holy Spirit, heat.' . . .The heat of the Spirit informs the whole of God and the whole of creation: 'The power of the Spirit's heat resides in everything (the whole of the created universe), with everything [the Spirit] is whole, yet entirely [whole] with the One (God), and is not cut off from the Radiance (Son), being mixed with it, [nor is the Spirit divided] from the Sun (Father), being mingled with it.'[xv]

St. Ephrem's metaphor of light and heat foreshadows the medieval hymns, mandalas, and theology of St. Hildegard of Bingen. In the 15th century Andrei Rublev painted *The Old Testament Trinity*, an icon of God, which has become quite famous. As you gaze into the icon, you are drawn to an open place about a low table, around which sit three relaxed figures. Upon the table sits a cup easily reached by any of the three. Each figure  rests peacefully and at ease in the presence of the other two. With heads inclined gently, yet deliberately, toward one another, there is a distinct air of mutual regard. A desire to drink in the presence of the others permeates the icon. These are figures ready to receive what the other has to give. Around this table each is utterly aware of the presence of the other, and each listens to the other with inclined ear and ready heart. One table, one cup, one mutual desire to listen to the other – born of eternal loving recognition of the holy present in all. Competition is as wholly absent as compassion is utterly present. Domination dissolves into equality. These three are one: one in open heart, one in listening mind, one in mutual love.

Rublev's icon is a vision for community life (an ecclesiology) as well as an understanding of divine life (a theology). Baptismal ministry begins with the inclined ear and open heart ready to receive in love the holy, which is the other. Baptismal ministry is thus a mutual ministry, which embodies One God, One Dance, One Community overflowing with gratefulness.

From within an integral sacramental vision, the Trinity, like the Incarnation, becomes a symbolic way of affirming the hope expressed in John's gospel that *all may be one, as you, Abba, are in me and I in you* (17.21) This unity is in no sense the exclusive oneness of mythic-literal Christianity. Whenever and wherever we accept the Spirit's invitation to live into the river of love that sustains all creation, we realize that we dwell in one another. There is no love not of God, and so there is no unity born of love not of God. The symbol of Trinity speaks to the eternal openness of life.

The open and embracing character of Trinitarian love in the icon is revealed also through the warm space between the two figures in the icon's foreground. Here there is forever a place at the table for another within the life of God. God *is* open embrace.[xvi]

The Johannine gospel declares that love is the Spirit that weaves our seemingly separate lives into a common fabric of community. Love draws a couple together to unite in partnership and family – united around birth and death, meal and story. These concrete and mundane activities are the very flesh of divine love lived. And love lived is Spirit weaving Trinitarian wholeness and communion. If we attend closely to how it is we not only survive but thrive, such wholeness is never realized in isolation but in community. Even when alone we are One. To live is to dwell in others as they dwell in us. One God. One Dance. One Community overflowing with gratefulness.

GOD AND "SATAN": CHRISTIAN RECONCILIATION

If we keep in mind the wisdom distilled from St. Ephrem that "error enters in when one person claims that his spiritual interpretation is the only one possible . . .," then the Holy Source invites us to discover ways to *passionately encourage* ongoing liturgical renewal that revitalizes baptismal ministry. Jesus offers some seminal wisdom in *The Gospel of Mary of Magdala* to guide our work, inviting us to lead with generosity:

> Go then, preach the good news about the Realm. Do not lay down any rule beyond what I determined for you, nor promulgate law like the lawgiver, or else you might be dominated by it."[xvii]

Just as we transcend the inadequate mythic-literal theologies of Incarnation and Trinity (not to mention the Genesis stories), so too we can recognize the symbolic and spiritual meaning in the language of satan and sin used by the church. Because the Holy Word is graciously fecund, we search for ways to move beyond the confines of literalism, be it with the Scriptures or *The Book of Common Prayer*. We seek words that speak clearly, meaningfully, and truthfully, about the enormously destructive power of evil in our lives.

I have rediscovered the traditional desert language of the passions/vices that the early fathers and mothers, East and West, used to name sin with powerful specificity. Avarice (greed), sloth, gluttony, anger, pride, envy, fear, lust – these are the passions identified by the early church as our experience of the blinding force of sin. *Ignorance of being created in the image of God is common to them all*. From these passions emerged what our tradition would later identify as the "seven deadly sins" (immortalized by Dante and Chaucer). Our baptismal transfiguration in Christ is the conversion (*metanoia*) of these sinful passions into their gracious virtues. The One Dance unfolds.

We need to develop prayers and liturgies that tell anew the ancient truth of Genesis that all are created in the image and invited to become the very likeness of God. These prayers and liturgies must have the power to bear us beyond the ego's tendency, when afraid, to demonize others. Such prayer and liturgy is essential to a baptismal ministry that affirms Christ in all persons and seeks justice and peace and reconciliation in God's creation.

The reason that such reconciliation is possible is boldly described by Meister Eckhart, who saw everyone as the sacred word of God, in whom Christ the Word lives. This vision of a thoroughly blessed creation led him to understand the reason for the Incarnation in a new way, where each of us is an "only begotten Son, and…no less."

AN INTEGRAL SACRAMENTAL VISION

What we are seeking to develop are prayers and liturgies that embody what I would describe as an integral sacramental vision of creation.[xviii] This sacramental vision has deep roots in our ancient catholic and mystic heritage and it offers a path through the modern and post-modern divorce of the sacred and the secular. This integral sacramental vision weaves a path for renewing our liturgy in such a way that it embodies a rediscovery of the Divine Center that is the Holy Source of all baptismal ministry.

Mutual Ministry Invites Us to **Taste** God Everywhere

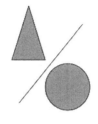  

God is above All   All is God   All is God and of God

An integral sacramental vision *invites us to taste God everywhere*. Here we move beyond the Anselmian theism which separates God from creation; we move beyond an overly simplified pantheism that would collapse the transcendent into the sum of the parts; we become saturated with a sacramental view that re-integrates sacred and secular, for all creation exists only to the degree it manifests God.

> God is more in me
> than if the whole sea
> could in a sponge wholly contained be.[xix]

Mutual Ministry Invites Us To **See** God in Everything

Beyond dualities of Sacred | Secular

Supernatural
Natural

to   Creation as Sacrament

This integral vision *invites us to see God in everything*. Here we move beyond the dualities of sacred/secular and supernatural/natural, which have been driving post-Enlightenment western culture, into a re-integrated sacramental worldview. History, as it is, is supernatural, for all things exist only insofar as God exists in and as them. History is epiphanic.

> In the infinity of the skies
> In the free flashing of lightning
> In whirling elemental winds
> You are God.
> In the impenetrable mists of dark clouds
> In the wild gusts of lashing rain
> In the ageless rocks of the sea
> You are God and I bless you.
> You are in all things
> And contained by no thing.
> You are the Life of all life
> And beyond every name.
> You are God and in the eternal mystery
> I praise you.[xx]

Mutual Ministry Invites Us
To **Know** Ourselves **as** Community

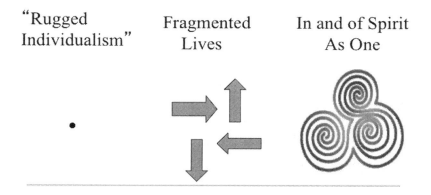

An integral sacramental vision *invites us to know ourselves as community*. Here we move beyond Modernity's ideology of the "rugged individual"; we move beyond Post-modernity's ideology of fragmented particularity; we recover and renew the wisdom of the ancient catholic tradition that all is in and of the Spirit as one.

All things come of thee, O Lord;
and of thine own have we given thee.
1 Chron. 29.14b

Mutual Ministry Invites Us to Move From Fear to **Trust**

Hierarchy that Dominates

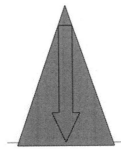

Hierarchy that Empowers (w)Holarchy

An integral sacramental vision *invites us to move from fear of God and creation to a basic trust in a Divine ever-present and dynamic*, which empowers each of us, as words of God, to live creatively within the Word. An integral sacramental vision *invites us to be transformed from the image into the very likeness of God*: Trinitarian communities characterized by the Gospel revelation that "friendship" lies at the heart of liturgy and ministry.

> Either we acknowledge that
> God is in all things
> or we have lost the basis for seeing
> God in anything.[xxi]

Liturgy & Mutual Ministry
Recovering At-One-Ment & Resurrection Paradise

Within an integral sacramental vision, liturgy, like baptismal ministry, is essentially our communal act of gratitude and praise to the Holy Source for our gracious and salvific At-one-ment, revealed in Christ Resurrected.

I believe that we find ourselves in a gracious moment where it is possible to transcend the bounds of an inadequate mythic-literal atonement theology, by recovering the fullness of our tradition and seeking creative ways to inculturate it in the 21st century. We reform our liturgy with the awareness that Resurrection Paradise and not dehumanizing crucifixion drew the Christians of the first millennium into worship. Brock and Parker argue that the first crucifix to luridly depict a suffering Christ, which makes Roman death central to Christianity, is found for the first time only in the 11th century. Of course, there are depictions of Jesus on a cross prior to this time, such as Christus Rex and the image carved of Jesus on the carved wood panel from the doors of the Basilica of Santa Sabina in the 4th century, among others,[xxii] but these are quite distinct from the later medieval "realistic" depictions of a suffering Christ crucifix. Here are some sobering words from *Saving Paradise: How Christianity Traded Love of This World for Crucifixion and Empire.*

> With Anselm's theology of atonement, the Incarnation's sole purpose was to drive relentlessly to the act of dying... Though he forbade his own monks from joining the Crusades, Anselm's doctrine of the atonement gave support for holy war. Christians were exhorted to imitate Christ's self-offering in the cause of God's justice. When authorities in the church called for vengeance, they did so on God's behalf. As Anselm wrote, "When earthly rulers exercise vengeance justifiably, the one who is really exercising it is the One who established them in authority for this very purpose."

> Anselm even fails to mention it [the resurrection] in [his book] *Why God Became Man.*

> [B]y the eleventh century, the church's rituals had virtually reversed the traditions of Cyril's fourth-century Jerusalem. Instead of mourning the Crucifixion once a year and marking the Resurrection daily, the Resurrection slowly receded in importance."

Anselm's theology and piety crystallized the religious foundation of the Crusades. "Peace by the blood of the Cross."[xxiii]

Now is the time for prayers and liturgies that seek to tell anew the ancient wisdom of paradise and empower us to move beyond "Peace by the blood of the Cross." These reformed liturgies substantially change the meaning of the call that we have to seek and serve Christ in all persons, to love our neighbors as ourselves, to strive for justice and peace among all people, and to respect the dignity of every human being.

Unfortunately, to say the least, Anselm's mythic-literal theology helped to provide justification for Christendom to embark on its first pogroms against the Jews of Europe. Soon after, the church found in the crucifix symbolic justification for the persecution of the Muslims of the holy land. The memory of the reign of God as paradise seemed lost. The memory of the Living Christ as the heart and soul of Christian prayer and liturgy seemed lost. Just as Jesus had to be killed in order to satisfy God's need for atonement, so too others had to pay with their lives for the affront of being judged "infidels."

Within an integral sacramental vision, liturgy embodies the ancient wisdom of why Jesus is Christ – because as God's love incarnate, death can neither contain nor destroy him (nor us). One God. One Dance. One Community overflowing with gratefulness.

Once again, the implications for the meaning of the promises of the baptismal covenant are quite profound. Even in the face of Roman crucifixion, Jesus remains constant to the Beloved who is eternally faithful to him. For the first Christians, who do not even speak of original sin, Jesus is killed not because God demands it; not because God needs it; not because God delights in it. Jesus is killed because Rome cannot tolerate the uncompromising love of the Incarnate One, manifested in healing and in table fellowship that is radically open to all. The symbolic language of resurrection reveals that we are One in life with God. One God. The resurrection also reveals that death, even one as horrific as crucifixion, cannot annihilate the Holy Word. Early eucharistic prayers never mention the crucifixion, because of its inhuman brutality. The One Dance of communal gratefulness continues.

An integral sacramental vision explores ways to give liturgical expression to the holy wisdom of Julian of Norwich: "All will be well." All will indeed be well for Julian because all are saved by God whose love and forgiveness are truly infinite. As Maggie Ross writes, "Julian of Norwich sums up the entire tradition. She repeatedly asks Christ, 'what is sin?' But

Christ tells her that he cannot even see sin; he can only see what is like himself, which is us, and all that is needed is to 'seek into the beholding.'" Julian's theology of redemption echoes that of Gregory of Nyssa, who in his *Life of Moses* "emphasizes universal and infinite resurrection as part of 'the very necessity of things.'" [xxiv]

An integral sacramental vision reclaims the wisdom theology of the Eastern Church that God became human so that we might become god. Jesus embodies the divine paradise which is the reign of God here and now and which reaches utter fullness beyond death. Themes of paradise grace the walls of the churches of the first millennium because all Christians are saints who exist solely for the purpose of the pilgrim journey of faith: created in the image of God, we are to become God's very likeness. We are words of the Word. The church fathers and mothers, East and West, as well as the medieval mystics, continually describe our journey of faith as a *theosis*: a human divinization. "I consider filiation of God to be reckoned as nothing else than deification, which, in Greek is also called *theosis*." (Nicholas Cusa)

Because the Beloved is the Alpha and Omega, the Source and the End, of all creation; and because we live, move, and have our being in a Font of boundless love; an integral sacramental vision recognizes that we live in a world in which every manifestation of truth, beauty, and goodness comes from God and leads to God and is thus sacred and holy. The very nature and dynamic of life itself is Trinitarian: all comes from the Holy Source, and we return all with hearts of gratefulness. One *kenotic* (ego-empty) Dance of gratefulness.

An integral sacramental vision invites us to reconsider our liturgical language and symbols as well as the meaning of our work with people from other faith traditions. Liturgy and ministry need to embody lived interfaith dialogue. For an integral sacramental vision, we cannot help but guard as sacred the many different paths into the Beloved, the Font of all Life. Our liturgy and ministry need to reflect hearts that are as ready to hear the good news from God's people of faiths, as they are to proclaim the Christian Gospel. The very goodness of the Gospel asks no less. We are called to become those who heal false divisions, celebrate our diversity, and pursue our common mission. This baptismal ministry of healing is the way of Jesus.

An integral sacramental vision invites us to create liturgies that remind, teach, and guide us in the way of being *kenotic* followers of Jesus. We develop language and ritual that help us to release our egoic pride and territoriality and receive the divine reaching out to us from others. We explore how are liturgies can better communicate the truth that

> ... 'the way' that John speaks of is not about believing doctrines about Jesus. Rather, 'the way' is what we see incarnate in Jesus: the path of death and resurrection as the way to rebirth in God. According to John, this is the only way – . . . it is 'the way' spoken of by all the major religions of the world. Dying and rising is the way. Thus Jesus is 'the Way' – the way become flesh. Rather than being the unique revelation of a way known only in him, his life and death are the incarnation of a universal way known in all of the enduring religions.[xxv]

Liturgical Resources

A downloadable file and license with permission to reproduce and use the following resources in worship is available from the publisher.

www.LeaderResources.org
800-941-2218

COLLECTS
Year A

ADVENT

FIRST SUNDAY OF ADVENT
ISAIAH 2:1-5
PSALM 122
ROMANS 13:11-14
MATTHEW 24:36-44

Presider: The Lord is with you.
Asse*m*bly: And also with you.
Presider: Let us pray together:
**God of Faithfulness,
in You alone is the promise of life:
be our courage,**
    as we climb the mountain of truth;
be our constancy,
    as we beat swords into ploughshares;
be our compassion,
    as we mold spears into pruning hooks;
be our companion,
    as we never again train for war.
**Be our life, through Christ,
the Promised One,
Who is ever with us. Amen.**

SECOND SUNDAY OF ADVENT
ISAIAH 11:1-10
PSALM 72:1-2, 7-8, 10-11, 12-13
ROMANS 15:4-13
MATTHEW 3:1-12

Flaming Breath of the Beloved,
burn away the chaff of restless thoughts and fearful passions,
that our trusting bodies might rest peacefully in You.
Root our lives,
stem, branch and trunk,
in the fertile Ground of your abiding compassion.
Deeply nourish our souls, so that –
  from your Breath alone
    we drink the Spirit of wisdom and understanding;
  from your Breath alone
    we drink the Spirit of counsel and strength;
  from your Breath alone
    we drink the Spirit of knowledge and reverence. Amen.

THIRD SUNDAY OF ADVENT
ISAIAH 35:1-10
PSALM 146:4-9
JAMES 5:7-10
MATTHEW 11:2-11

Beloved,
through your forgiving Heart
runs the Sacred Path of life.
The One who is come,
Jesus,
  is your Heart,
    your Path,
      incarnate for all creation.
Open our eyes to behold your Beauty.
Unstop our ears to receive your Voice.
Loose our tongues to sing your Joy.
Mend our broken bodies to dance your Song.
So that we,
  as the body of Christ,
    may be your Path of life,
      this very day,
        for the world. Amen.

Fourth Sunday of Advent
Isaiah 7:10-16
Psalm 80:1-7,16-18
Romans 1:1-7
Matthew 1:18-25

Holy One of Israel
in You all life is conceived and born;
prepare our hearts
to received the eternal gift
of Christ –
    born as Jesus of Nazareth;
till the soil of our souls
to bear the birth within us
of Immanuel;
for You are
God with us,
now and forever. Amen.

Christmas

Feast of the Nativity
Isaiah 9:2-7
Psalm 96
Titus 2:11-14
Luke 2:1-14(15-20)

Welcome Jesus, our humble, gentle, Savior,
welcome to Bethlehem
where we have loved and fought
and longed for the peace the world can never give.
We ask for your peace, your love, your gentleness,
and the courage to live that way.
Child of God, child of Mary and Joseph,
born in the stable at Bethlehem,
may we know you as born in us this day.
That through us the world may know
the wonder of your boundless love. Amen.

CHRISTMAS EVE LATE
ISAIAH 62:6-12
PSALM 97
TITUS 3:4-7
LUKE 2(1-7), 8-20

Beloved God:
Eternal Evening Star,
Deliverer of life,
Redeemer of hope,
Bearer of Kindness and Love;
You name us – "Sought After";
You proclaim us – "A City Not Forsaken."
Our hearts sing and sing and sing your praise.
For this night, with all creation,
we are born anew
in Christ Jesus,
Your eternal Word become flesh. Amen.

FIRST SUNDAY AFTER CHRISTMAS
ISAIAH 61:10-62:3
PSALM 147
GALATIANS 3:23-25; 4:4-7
JOHN 1:1-18

God of Light and Life:
your Light
shatters the darkness;
your Light
shows the way;
your Light *is* Life.
In your Light we are born,
like Jesus,
> not simply of flesh,
> not only of human will,
but of God.
And so our voices praise You,
through Christ our Light. Amen.

SECOND SUNDAY AFTER CHRISTMAS
JEREMIAH 31:7-14
PSALM 84
EPHESIANS 1:3-6,15-19A
LUKE 2:41-52

Living Water,
You are forever our Mother and Father
and we your firstborn –
conceived in Christ, before the world began:
    may mercy gently mold our hearts;
    may forgiveness open wide our arms;
    may wisdom bring rich knowledge of You.
So that as the waters run home to the sea,
all that we are
    and all that we have
        return in full
            to You. Amen.

EPIPHANY

EPIPHANY
ISAIAH 60:1-6
PSALM 72
EPHESIANS 3-1
MATTHEW 2:1-12

Eternal Day Star,
You are the Wisdom
for our life's journey.
You strengthen our hearts
to remain constantly set on you.
You settle our minds
to know true gold amidst a world
of glittering falsehood.
You assure our souls
that the path of Christ's compassion
is the way, the truth, and the life. Amen

First Sunday after Epiphany – Baptism of Jesus

Isaiah 42:1-9
Psalm 29
Acts 10:34-43
Matthew 3:13-17

God of Light and Wisdom,
your Love cascades over creation.
May we be so thoroughly immersed
in these fiery waters
that we know all peoples,
all creatures,
as your Own,
as your Beloved.
May we be your servant,
like Jesus,
who in freedom and peace
faithfully brings forth true justice. Amen

Second Sunday after Epiphany

Isaiah 49:1-7
Psalm 40
1 Corinthians 1:1-9
John 1:29-42

God of Light and Wisdom:
May we hold in trust
the questioning mind,
the searching heart,
and the thirsting soul.
May we guard as sacred
the many different paths into you,
The Font of all Life.
May we be as ready to hear the good news
from your people of other denominations and faiths,
as we are to proclaim the gospel;
through the healing Spirit of Christ. Amen

Third Sunday after Epiphany

Isaiah 9:1-4
Psalm 27
1 Corinthians 1:10-18
Matthew 4:12-23

God of Light and Wisdom:
in Jesus of Nazareth,
You have caused a great light to shine –
> on those living in the shadow of fear;
> on those living in the shadow of deceit;
> on those living in the shadow of anger.

Soften the hardness of our hearts.
Release the doors of our minds,
so that we know the kingdom of heaven
is at hand.
And filled with the Spirit,
we come and follow the way of Jesus. Amen

~OR

God of Light and Wisdom,
You shine brilliant as a diamond
from within the deep shadows.
Strong, steady and sure, is your Light,
strengthening our heart
for the journey into the Land Beyond the Jordan:

> beyond the shadow of judgment
> beyond the shadow of anger
> beyond the shadow of rejection.

Draw us even beyond the shadow of belonging,
and form us into Citadels of Christ:

> brilliant jewels of infinite kindness
> dwelling in the Light of your face. Amen.

Fourth Sunday after Epiphany

MICAH 6:1-8
PSALM 15
1 CORINTHIANS 1:18-31
MATTHEW 5:1-12

God of Light and Wisdom,
our exhausted hearts plead before your Holy Mountain.
We seek your face.
We climb and climb and climb,
    dropping with each step
        further down into the foundation of our soul.
Until ----- You.
You are "I Am."
    I Am the exhaustion.
    I Am the mountain.
    I Am the climb.
    I Am your heart, your mind, your body, your strength.
With our soul your "I Am,"
may we behold each face as You,
and be a welcome refuge for a weary world. Amen.

Fifth Sunday after Epiphany

ISAIAH 58:1-9A,(9B-12)
PSALM 112:1-9,(10)
1 CORINTHIANS 2:1-12,(13-16)
MATTHEW 5:13-20

God of Light and Wisdom,
we long to be seen by You,
whose gentle eyes bathe us in kindness;
we long to be noticed by You,
whose loving Presence we already are.
Throw open wide the eyes of our soul to see that
    when we break the yoke of a sister's grief,
        You are here, now;
    when we listen to the yearning of a brother's heart,
        You are here, now.
As the Reign of God dawns fresh this very day,
may we notice that in each touch and word
we unfold as You, here and now. Amen.

SIXTH SUNDAY AFTER EPIPHANY
DEUTERONOMY 30:15-20
PSALM 119:1-8
1 CORINTHIANS 3:1-9
MATTHEW 5:21-37

God of Light and Wisdom,
for far too long our hearts have remained
fearfully and fitfully tethered to threatening commandments.
For far too long our minds have remained
frozen to conventional obedience dreading the curse of condemnation.
May the Beloved's voice echo within the chambers of our heart
like that of a Lover calling again and again and again:
> I am yours. You are mine. We are one.
> I am yours. You are mine. We are one.

When our hearts become confused and stray,
You, our Beloved, draw us home.
Whether the journey of return is
short or long,
convoluted or straight.
You bring us home
freely and fully,
Yours. Amen.

SEVENTH SUNDAY AFTER EPIPHANY
LEVITICUS 19:1-2,9-18
PSALM 119:33-40
1 CORINTHIANS 3:10-11,16-23
MATTHEW 5:38-48

God of Light and Wisdom,
your Presence so permeates unfolding creation
that You invite us to discover Perfection
in the very cracks and crevices of our shattered world.
Unbind the judgments that gnarl and harden our body:
> Teach us the Perfection
>> that empties our heart of hatred for those who threaten us.
>
> Teach us the Perfection
>> that frees our mind from judgment of those we do not understand.
>
> Teach us the Perfection
>> of being as vulnerable as Jesus on the cross,
>> laid open to your Wisdom
>> that reaches to feed us
>> this very moment. Amen.

Eighth Sunday after Epiphany
ISAIAH 49:8-16A
PSALM 131
1 CORINTHIANS 4:1-5
MATTHEW 6:24-34

God of Light and Wisdom,
so often our minds are congested thick with worry.
Anxious,
we become prisoners of our own plans,
running down roads that end in a maze of darkness.
Show yourself to us this moment,
arising as the clear and full Moon,
pressing your golden face against ours,
seizing our hearts as a Lover.
Now,
our minds are clear,
and we long for nothing of this world.
We desire only the taste
of Christ. Amen.

Last Sunday after Epiphany
EXODUS 24:12-18
PSALM 99
2 PETER 1:16-21
MATTHEW 17:1-9

God of Light and Wisdom:
You call us to ascend the mountain
and wait for You.
Be our strength to climb
the fears and doubts of our heart.
Be our courage
to be engulfed by the cloud of your glory.
Be our patience
to receive the all-consuming fire of your Presence.
And burn away the chaff that hides
the glory of our Belovedness in You;
in the Spirit of Christ we pray. Amen.

LENT

ASH WEDNESDAY
ISAIAH 58:1-12
PSALM 103
2 CORINTHIANS 5:20B—6:10
MATTHEW 6:1-6, 16-21

Beloved God,
You are present within us
as a fire burning in our hearts:
> burn away the shame that imprisons our souls;
> burn away the rage that drives us to vengeance;
> burn away the fear that despairs of your love.
Leave nothing buried in our ashes,
but hearts alive to You in Christ. Amen.

FIRST SUNDAY IN LENT
GENESIS 2:15-17, 3:1-7
PSALM 32
ROMANS 5:12-19
MATTHEW 4:1-11

God of the desert,
for knowledge of You alone do we ache:
feed our souls with words from your mouth;
strengthen our hearts with the kiss of your holy breath;
receive our bodies
as we fall down in adoration and worship
of You alone. Amen.

Second Sunday in Lent
Genesis 12:1-4a
Psalm 121
Romans 4:1-5,13-17
John 3:1-17

God of the desert,
Your Spirit gives birth to all creation,
yet, we seem to know You not.
Lead us on the journey into the reign of God
where our souls behold the eternal truth:
> our mind is born of your Spirit;
> our heart is born of your Spirit;
> our body is born of your Spirit. Amen.

Third Sunday in Lent
Exodus 17:1-7
Psalm 95
Romans 5:1-11
John 4:5-42

God of the desert,
strike the rock of our hearts
so that we might be a people –
hungering only to do your will with each person we meet;
thirsting only to receive your words from the mouth of a stranger;
knowing for ourselves your compassionate path
as the only way of Holy Hope. Amen.

Fourth Sunday in Lent
1 Samuel 16:1-13
Psalm 23
Ephesians 5:8-14
John 9:1-41

God of the desert,
your light pierces the darkest night:
draw us into the luminous depths of Siloam,
consecrating us in Christ;
dispel the blinding darkness of deceit,
opening the eyes of our heart to see as Christ;
pierce us thru and thru,
that we might become nothing
but luminous vessels of Christ. Amen.

Fifth Sunday in Lent
Ezekiel 37:1-14
Psalm 130
Romans 8:6-11
John 11:1-45

God of the desert,
Your Word is life:
when we cry,
    "our bones are dry";
when we lament,
    "our hope is gone."
Be now our strength
    to take away the stone of doubt.
Be now the Word
    that reaches out into the grave of our heart
    and calls forth new life. Amen.

Palm Sunday
Gathering – Liturgy of the Palms
Matthew 21:1-11
Psalm 118

Presider: Blessed is the King
    who comes in the name of the Lord.
Assembly: Peace in heaven and glory in the highest.
Presider: Let us pray together
  Sovereign of creation,
  You show us the path of life:
  hungry neither for honor nor glory,
  The Anointed One completely empties his heart;
  deceived neither by flattery nor promise,
  The Anointed One rests only in your presence.
  Release us from the fear of being forsaken,
  so that with the last breath
  our soul cries out,
  My Lord and my God. Amen.

Maundy Thursday – Sent to Serve

Exodus 12:1-4, (5-10), 11-14
Psalm 116:1, 10-17
1 Corinthians 11:23-26
John 13:1-17, 31b-35

Beloved,
life is a banquet
overflowing from the heart of your dance of Love.
On this night,
The Lover has annihilated Jesus.
Now Love alone remains,
who invites all to the table
spread upon the sea of generosity.
Freely, Love pours forth life.
This Soul is free, supremely free,
    in the stock,
        in all her branches
            and all the fruits of her braches.
Nothing but sweet flowing wine remains
and the Soul says:
Drink this, all of you:
This is my life Blood
a joyous Covenant from which flows
forgiveness of sin and life renewed.
Remember, you can be no less for me. Amen.

inspired by Marguerite Porete

See page 149 for the Maundy Thursday Liturgy

Good Friday – The Cycle of Suffering Ceases

Isaiah 52:13-53:12
Psalm 22
Hebrews 10:16-25
John's Passion

Presider: Blessed be the Beloved,
Assembly: **Forever and ever. Amen.**
Presider: Beloved God,
we, your very own,
created in your image
and called to become your likeness,
are blinded by our ignorance, fear, anger and greed.
This sinful veil blinds us
to your beauty embodied in neighbor and creation.
We stand before You
with your mercy raining down upon us,
washing over our lives with renewing forgiveness.
Be the grace that strengthens us to serve You
in newness of life,
to the glory of your name. **Amen**.

Presider: Let us pray together:
**Gracious God,
turn the gaze of our souls to
Jesus, the Beloved,
heart of our heart,
whose beauty was broken open upon the cross:
may Christ's arms embrace our broken lives;
may Christ's heart heal our tortured world;
and may the sinful veil
of ignorance, fear, anger and greed
be lifted from our eyes,
so that we might see
and fall into the Beloved's boundless mercy.
Amen.**

The Solemn Collects are on page 152 and the Liturgy is on page 151.
The Easter Vigil is on page 156.

Easter

Easter Sunday – Life Renewed

Jeremiah 31.1-6
Psalm 118: 1-2, 14-24
Acts 10: 34-43
Matthew 28:1-10

Presider: There is one Body and one Spirit;
Assembly: **There is one hope in God's call to us;**
Presider: One Lord, one Faith, one Baptism;
Assembly: **One God and Father of all.**
Presider: The Lord is with you.
Assembly: **And also with you.**
Presider: Let us pray together
In water are we conceived.
In water are we knit together in the Spirit.
Through the breaking of water are we born.
Through the drinking of water are we nourished.
You, O God, *are* **the living water:**
  wash over us, again and again and again,
that in Christ we might live as your
  daughters and sons,
and that with Christ as our heart
we might respect the dignity
  of every human being. Amen.

Second Sunday of Easter
Acts 2:14a, 22-32
Psalm 16
1 Peter 1:3-9
John 20:19-31

Presider: Alleluia. Christ is risen.
Assembly: **Christ is risen indeed. Alleluia.**
Presider: Alleluia. Christ is risen.
Assembly: **Christ is risen indeed. Alleluia.**
Presider: Alleluia. Christ is risen.
Assembly: **Christ is risen indeed. Alleluia.**
Presider: The Lord is with you.
Assembly: **And also with you.**
Presider : Let us pray together:
Blessed God of Holy Hope,
    in You alone are we reborn:
be the Hope that shows our minds
    the many paths of Life;
be the Hope that gladdens our hearts
    and frees our tongues to rejoice;
be the Hope that sends us forth in Christ's Spirit
    to be the peace we often cannot see;
in Christ's name we pray. Amen.

Third Sunday of Easter

Acts 2:14a,36-41
Psalm 11:1-3,10-17
1 Peter 1:17-23
Luke 24:13-35

Presider: Alleluia. Christ is risen.
Assembly: **Christ is risen indeed. Alleluia.**
Presider: Alleluia. Christ is risen.
Assembly: **Christ is risen indeed. Alleluia.**
Presider: Alleluia. Christ is risen.
Assembly: **Christ is risen indeed. Alleluia.**
Presider: The Lord is with you.
Assembly: **And also with you.**
Presider: Let us pray together:
**God of Holy Love,
your Presence quickens
our deadened hearts:
before the world's foundation
Love is your fiery seed
planted as the soul of life;
burn inside us this day,
turning our hearts to Christ,
the courageous Lamb
who reveals the way of freedom and life. Amen.**

Fourth Sunday of Easter

Acts 2:42-47
Psalm 23
1 Peter 2:19-25
John 10:1-10

Presider: Alleluia. Christ is risen.
Presider: Alleluia. Christ is risen.
Assembly: **Christ is risen indeed. Alleluia.**
Presider: Alleluia. Christ is risen.
Assembly: **Christ is risen indeed. Alleluia.**
Presider: Alleluia. Christ is risen.
Assembly: **Christ is risen indeed. Alleluia.**
Presider: The Lord is with you.
Assembly: **And also with you.**
Presider: Let us pray together:
**Faithful and Loving Shepherd,
You eternally receive Jesus
and reveal the crucified One as the gate of life:
surrounded by the shadow of death,
the cross is our courage to release fear;
suffering for the sake of justice and peace,
the cross is our courage to release retribution;
open our hearts
to break bread with all who hunger;
open our eyes
to see the gate of life as forever open;
receive our selves, our souls, our bodies,
that we may have life in You to the full. Amen.**

Fifth Sunday of Easter
Acts 7:55-60
Psalm 31:1-5,15-16
1 Peter 2:2-10
John 14:1-14

Presider: Alleluia. Christ is risen.
Assembly: **Christ is risen indeed. Alleluia.**
Presider: Alleluia. Christ is risen.
Assembly: **Christ is risen indeed. Alleluia.**
Presider: Alleluia. Christ is risen.
Assembly: **Christ is risen indeed. Alleluia.**
Presider: The Lord is with you.
Assembly: **And also with you.**
Presider: Let us pray together:
**God of Truth,
in Christ is the living stone
who shows us the Way, the Truth and the Life:
The Way of Christ
    is to commit our spirits to You;
The Truth of Christ
    is to know that in your heart are
    many dwelling places;
The Life of Christ
    is to taste You, Our God, as Good.
In gratitude we offer our praise –
    that hearts once hardened by fear into stone
    now pulsate with the compassion of Jesus.
    Amen.**

Sixth Sunday of Easter
Acts 17:22-31
Psalm 66
1 Peter 3:13-22
John 14:15-21

Presider: Alleluia. Christ is risen.
Assembly: **Christ is risen indeed. Alleluia.**
Presider: Alleluia. Christ is risen.
Assembly: **Christ is risen indeed. Alleluia.**
Presider: Alleluia. Christ is risen.
Assembly: **Christ is risen indeed. Alleluia.**
Presider: The Lord is with you.
Assembly: **And also with you.**
Presider: Let us pray together:
**Holy Spirit of Truth,
Breath of Life:
In You, we live and move and have our being;
in You, we have no fear;
You are in us, we are in You;
breathe into us now and reform our minds,
to know You as the One who gives everyone life;
breathe into us now and reform our hearts,
to embody your justice in a broken world.
To You alone we graciously return
all that we are:
mind, heart and body. Amen.**

Ascension
Acts 1:1-11
Psalm 47
Ephesians 1:15-23
Luke 24:44-53

Beloved God,
 Creator of All:
your Love alone is sovereign in our lives;
your Hope alone authors our path;
your Faith alone empowers our hearts;
May our hearts ascend with Christ
into your abiding Presence –
The Divine Sea of Compassion,
which fills heaven and earth. Amen.

ASCENSION & SEVENTH SUNDAY OF EASTER
ACTS 1:1-11
PSALM 66:8-20
1 PETER 3:13-22
JOHN 14:15-21

Abba,
You are the only true God,
whose glory alone resurrects Jesus,
and calls the Beloved home.
Now,
    this moment,
               our eyes ascend to You.
Fear no longer drives us down.
Hate no longer clenches our hearts.
Deceit no longer clouds our minds.
Christ has shattered theses stones of death.
You alone possess Jesus.
You alone possess us.
All that live belong to You
the only true God. Amen.

PENTECOST

FEAST OF PENTECOST
ACTS 2:1-21
PSALM 104
1 CORINTHIANS 12:3B-13
JOHN 20:19-23

Divine Spirit,
Infinite Wellspring,
all life arises from your depths:
You enfold in us,
we unfold in You;
You enflame our hearts with compassion;
You enlighten our minds with hope;
You inspire our bodies to trust that
forgiveness is the path of life;
as echoes of the deep,
send us forth as
Christ's peace in creation. Amen.

inspired by Nicholas Cusa and Catherine Keller

TRINITY SUNDAY
GENESIS 1:1-2:4A
PSALM 8
2 CORINTHIANS 13:11-13
MATTHEW 28:16-20

God of earth and sky,
fire and water, life and death,
You are the gracious Source
of all that is:
    from You,
        we receive creative minds;
    from You
        we receive beautiful bodies;
    from You
        we receive hearts woven of love;
this day, born anew of your Spirit,
we gratefully return
all we are to You:
our Life, our Hope, our Love. Amen.

inspired by Brother David Steindl-Rast

Proper 3
Isaiah 49:8-16a
Psalm 131
1 Corinthians 4:1-15
Matthew 6:24-34

Holy God,
your compassionate faithfulness
strengthens us for the journey of life:

> be the Hope that brings to light
> your eternal Presence within creation;
>
> be the Truth that stirs us to action,
> seeking first your Reign;
>
> be the Faith that calms our worrying minds,
> trusting in your Justice

to heal, renew, and sustain all life. Amen.

PROPER 4
DEUTERONOMY 11:18-21, 26-28
PSALM 31
ROMANS 1:16-17; 3:22B-28-31)
MATTHEW 7:21-29

God of Holy Hope,
your Spirit,
written upon our hearts and bodies,
draws us forth to restore life:

> transform our prideful hearts,
> teaching us the practice of true care;
>
> transform our fearful hearts,
> teaching us the practice of unwavering courage;
>
> transform our tired hearts,
> teaching us the practice of right action;

in the Spirit of Christ,
may we live as your Justice. Amen.

PROPER 5
HOSEA 5:15-6:6
PSALM 50
ROMANS 4:13-25
MATTHEW 9:9-13, 18-26

Beloved God,
You are Holy Love,
the power to raise up and call forth life:
return to us this day
> like the rains of spring that water the earth;

return to us this day
> as the hope against hope;

return to us this day,
> as the courage healing our hearts
> dead in sleep.

Call us forth into life this day,
where your desire becomes our
unbounded kindness towards others and our
knowledge of You. Amen.

Proper 6
EXODUS 19:2-8A
PSALM 100
ROMANS 5:1-8
MATTHEW 9:35-10:8, (9-23)

God of Holy Hope,
in your Spirit
deception is transformed into honesty.
You are the power who
carries us:
> when our hearts would restrict your love
> to cherish only ourselves;
> when our minds would claim
> only our traditions are cherished by You as holy;
your Spirit draws us beyond self-deception
and opens our hearts and minds to know
that the whole earth is yours and holy. Amen.

Proper 7
JEREMIAH 20:7-13
PSALM 69:8-11, (12-17), 18-20
ROMANS 6:1B-11
MATTHEW 10:24-39

Beloved God,
You are present within us
as a fire burning in our hearts:
> burn away the shame that imprisons our souls;
> burn away the rage that drives us to vengeance;
> burn away the fear that despairs of your love.
Leave nothing buried in our ashes,
but hearts alive to You in Christ. Amen.

Proper 8
Jeremiah 28:5-9
Psalm 89:1-4, 15-18
Romans 6:12-23
Matthew 10:40-42

Beloved God,
in your heart all are welcome to discover
the way of eternal life:

> when lust for power drives us relentlessly to control,
> You, as Holy Truth,
> awaken us to the peace of vulnerability;

> when craving for recognition renders us blind to others,
> You, as Holy Hope,
> awaken us to the tenderness of integrity;

> when lust renders us deadly numb to what matters,
> You, as Holy Love,
> awaken us to the justice of right action.

Be to us this day
The Heart of our heart,
so that without reserve
we might in Christ be stewards of justice,
who welcome all in peace. Amen.

Proper 9
Zechariah 9: 9-12
Psalm 145: 8-15
Romans 7: 15-25a
Matthew 11: 16-19, 25-30

Beloved Creator of heaven and earth
You are the Holy Wisdom guiding the unfolding of life:

> when we seek refuge in our clever minds,
> You invite us simply to return to our hearts;

> when we are drawn to the power of the chariot,
> You invite us gently to dwell in the sea of peace;

> when we are tired and weary from the burdens of life,
> You invite us wholly to rest in your humble heart.

Be to us this day the River of Life,
carrying all in Christ beyond the power of death. Amen.

Proper 10
ISAIAH 55:10-13
PSALM 65: (1-8), 9-14
ROMANS 8:1-11
MATTHEW 13:1-9, 18-23

Beloved,
Ground of all life:

> in You our hearts are fertile and fruitful,
> we break into cries of joy;
>
> in You our bodies whirl about divinely drunk,
> we clap our hands in praise;
>
> in You our minds drink fully your flowing Word,
> we enjoy the sweet taste of freedom.

You are the Ground from which all life springs,
call us forth in Christ this day. Amen.

Proper 11
ISAIAH 44:6-8
PSALM 86:11-17
ROMANS 8:12-25
MATTHEW 13:24-30, 36-43

God of Freedom,
your steadfast breath is our beginning and end:

> in You is the Strength to move beyond
> the fearful trap of judgment;
>
> in You is the Power to break through
> the enslavement of condemnation;
>
> in You is the Loving-Kindness that burns away
> the chaff of our anxiety and anger –

opening our souls to rest forever in
the gentle, cool, breeze of Compassion. Amen.

inspired by The Jesus Sutras

Proper 12
1 Kings 3:5-12
Psalm 119: 129-136
Romans 8:26-39
Matthew 13:31-33, 44-52

Holy Wisdom,
for you our hearts long
with groanings too deep for words.
Open wide our bodies
   to know that all share in the image of the Only Begotten.
Open wide our minds
   to know that nothing can separate us from your love.
Open wide our hearts
   to know the pearl of life, the kingdom of heaven,
   is the land of our very own soul. Amen.

Proper 13
Isaiah 55:1-5
Psalm 145:8-9, 15-22
Romans 9:1-5
Matthew 14:13-21

Holy One,
You are everlasting life:
we seek a deserted place –
      to be alone with You;
we hunger for your Presence –
      to know only You;
we thirst for your kiss –
      to love only You;
lure our longing hearts to You –
      open and empty;
that your Presence completely fill us and
become our own heart. Amen.

Proper 14
1 Kings 19:9-18
Psalm 85:8-13
Romans 10:5-15
Matthew 14:22-33

Beloved One,
You are God Omnipotent:

>when knees buckle to the god of isolation,
>You are our strength to depend on community;
>
>when hearts fall to lust for control,
>You are our strength to become innocent;
>
>when minds succumb to the winds of fear,
>You are our strength of Holy Trust.

Instruct us in the power of Christ's compassion,
a tenacious loving-kindness that never fails. Amen.

Proper 15
Isaiah 56:1, 6-8
Psalm 67
Romans 11:1-2a, 29-32
Matthew 15: (10-20), 21-28

Adonai,
You alone are Sovereign of Creation:

>when our mouths would defile one another;
>when our eyes would be blind to your Presence;
>transform our hearts in Christ;

so that we might receive the one who is before us,
>not as our prejudice would judge,
>but as the very Presence of You,
>The Just and the Living God. Amen.

Proper 16
ISAIAH 51:1-6
PSALM 138
ROMANS 12:1-8
MATTHEW 16:13-20

Beloved Adonai,
You are the living Rock
from which all life is cut:

>though the earth wear out;
>though creatures wither and die –
>our hearts are hewn of You.

Flow into us this day,
>forever forming us as one body in Christ.

Flow into us this day,
>renewing our minds
>to know your Reign
>as the bedrock of freedom from all bondage. Amen.

Proper 17
JEREMIAH 15:1-21
PSALM 26:1-8
ROMANS 12:9-21
MATTHEW 16:21-28

God Omnipotent,
in Christ is the true eternal nature of
your power and our souls revealed:

>mercy, not vengeance, is the path of life;
>forgiveness, not retribution, is the way of salvation;
>serenity, not wrath, returns our souls to You.

You are the Power inviting us
  to release our hunger for the world's approval.
You are the Power strengthening us
  to release the passions that drive our hearts.
You are the Power generating all life,
  asking only that we release ourselves
  to You. Amen.

Proper 18
Ezekiel 33:7-11
Psalm 119:33-40
Romans 13:8-14
Matthew 18:15-20

Beloved One,
in Jesus of Nazareth you are manifest as
Holy Love.
In Love, we realize the gracious beauty of our soul –
    we are without shame.
In Love, we are bound by an ocean of mercy –
    we are all welcome at the table.
In Love, we know the Truth that sets us free –
    we are perfectly one in God.
May Holy Love so infuse our hearts
that our minds see your Presence, All in all. Amen.

Proper 19
Genesis 50:15-21
Psalm 103: (1-7), 8-13
Romans 14:1-12
Matthew 18:21-35

Gracious God,
Endless Ocean of Soothing Mercy:

      when our minds would doubt
      our own worth,
      in Christ we discover our eternal beauty;

      when our anxious hearts would fear You
      as a seat of judgment,
      in Christ we know your Presence as
      forgiveness without end.

Loosen the resentment that entangles our weary minds,
teaching our hearts to die to life in Christ. Amen.

Proper 20
JONAH 3:10-4:11
PSALM 145
PHILIPPIANS 1:21-30
MATTHEW 20:1-16

Blessed Creator,
from whom and in whom all life flows:

> when our hearts grow jealous of your love
> for the just and unjust alike;

> when our hearts grow envious of your prodigal generosity
> for the first as well as the last;

may Christ be our gracious guide
reminding us that whenever we return our hearts to You,
tenderness, compassion and rich kindness
are there to receive *us*. Amen.

Proper 21
ISAIAH 5:1-7
PSALM 80
PHILIPPIANS 3:4B-14
MATTHEW 21:33-46

Sovereign God,
every living soul belongs to You
and rests within your kindness.
Release our hearts from the vanity
　　of competition for your favor.
Release our minds from clinging to the conceit
　　that our worth surpasses others.
Turn us wholly to Christ
who reveals the path of life –

> become completely empty of all pretension
> and hear only your call to loving-kindness. Amen.

Proper 22
Isaiah 5:1-7
Psalm 80
Philippians 3:4b-14
Matthew 21:33-46

Beloved Creator,
we are your vineyard,
the holy ground
in which You live and move and have being.
May your Spirit
till the soil of our souls so that
suffering is no more:

> justice, not bloodshed,
> becomes the fruit of our labor;
>
> forgiveness, not judgment,
> becomes the offering of our heart;
>
> hope, not despair,
> becomes the message of our lives;

in Christ, we pray. Amen.

Proper 23
Isaiah 25:1-9
Psalm 23
Philippians 4:1-9
Matthew 22:1-14

Beloved One,
we give thanks
that your grace
always precedes and follows us.
May our hearts so live from your abiding Presence
that all our works become signs of your compassion;
through Jesus Christ,
who lives and reigns with you in the Spirit, One God,
now and forever. Amen.

Proper 24

Exodus 33.12-23
Psalm 99
1 Thessalonians 1.1-10
Matthew 22.15-22

Beloved Teacher,
we rejoice
that You give birth in Christ to all creatures,
and that your Spirit quickens the universe.
Draw us into the furnace of your Spirit
burning away the hard edges of blinding fear.
Anoint the eyes our hearts
with your love,
that we might fully see and freely
give to God what is God's –
everything. Amen.

Proper 25

Leviticus 19:1-2, 15-18
Psalm 1
1 Thessalonians 2:1-8
Matthew 22:34-46

Holy One,
all rivers run to the Sea.
What is Divine righteousness,
    but compassion for each face of God?
What is Divine judgment,
    but the rule of forgiveness in our lives?
What is Divine holiness,
    but the flow of love into tender yet tenacious
    lives of justice?
May we, as Christ's body,
flow fully into You,
holy into Holy. Amen.

Proper 26
MICAH 3:5-12
PSALM 43
1 THESSALONIANS 2:9-13
MATTHEW 23:1-12

Blessed Creator,
for You our hearts long.
Be to us
    the Holy Truth in whom we rest.
Be to us
    the gentle Sovereign of our souls.
Be to us
    the Strength to love until we lie spent.
Be to us
    our very will,
    empty,
    and full of Christ. Amen.

All Saints
REVELATION 7:9-17
PSALM 34_1-10,22
1 JOHN 3: 1-3
MATTHEW 5:1-12

Blessed One,
as your abiding Presence we your creatures are One –
a vibrant mystical tapestry woven of Love.
    When any child hungers,
        the pang is ours.
    When any sister grieves,
        the mourning is ours.
    When any brother is bruised,
        the sorrow is ours.
    When any creature is glad,
        the dance is ours.
We are the blessed company of the saints,
whose only joy is knowing and loving You. Amen.

Proper 27
Amos 5:18-24
Psalm 70
1 Thessalonians 4:13-18
Matthew 25:1-13

God of light and
God of darkness,
when we are foolish and feel the door to You is shut,
the abiding truth of Christ awakens us:
You alone are the wellspring of life –
    your healing justice flows like a river from our souls;
You alone are the lamp of our hearts –
    the oil of your love burns bright our way.
Settle us into the unfailing stream of your serenity,
this day and always. Amen.

Proper 28
Zephaniah 1:7,12-18
Psalm 90:1-8,(9-11),12
1 Thessalonians 5:1-11
Matthew 25:14-30

Gracious God,
Holy Wisdom,
draw us beyond the false knowledge of our fear:
    in fear, we would know You as a god of wrath;
    in fear, we would know You as a god of devastation;
    in fear, we would know You as a god who is ruthless.
Dispel our ignorance and guide our hearts
to know
that whether awake or asleep
Holy Peace and Love are always in us,
as we live together in Christ. Amen.

inspired by Julian of Norwich

Proper 29
Ezekiel 34:11-16,20-24
Psalm 95:1-7a
Ephesians 1:15-23
Matthew 25:31-46

Sovereign God,
Holy and Immortal One,
guide our souls to know that
      far above the sovereignty of our fears;
      far above the authority of our prejudices;
      far above the dominion of our condemnations;
      and far above the power of all our judgments
is the Truth of the Abiding Presence of Christ –
      whenever we care for the least among us,
      we know You in our midst. Amen.

Year B
Advent

First Sunday of Advent
Isaiah 64:1-9
Psalm 80:1-7,16-18
1 Corinthians 1:3-9
Mark 13:24-37

Promised One,
Holy One of Faith:
in our confusion
>we would fear for our salvation;
>we would be captive to our anxiety;
>we would confuse You with our lost and angry hearts.

Awaken us to your saving Presence
>and lift the veil of ignorance from our minds.

Awaken us to know today is the promised day
>and this very hour is the moment of salvation.

Now, You come into our hearts.
Now, we become a Just and Compassionate people. Amen.

Second Sunday of Advent
Isaiah 40:1-11
Psalm 85:1-2,8-13
2 Peter 3:8-15a
Mark 1:1-8

Promised One,
Holy One of Faith:
You speak tenderly
>to Jerusalem's heart;

You clear a path
>through the wilderness of her memories;

You make a straight road
>through the desert of her plans.

May the fire of your love
burn away all false hopes of heaven,
and create a new heaven and earth
in the hearts and lives of the just. Amen.

Third Sunday of Advent
ISAIAH 61:1-4,8-11
PSALM 126
1 THESSALONIANS 5:16-24
JOHN 1:6-8,19-28

Promised One,
Holy One of Faith:
Your Spirit rests upon us,
for You have anointed us –
> to bring good news to the poor;
> to proclaim liberty to the captive;
> to set free those in prison;
> to announce a year of divine favor.

May the Light of your Spirit
illumine all humanity,
so that dwelling in Christ –
> we repair ruined lives;
> we rebuild broken spirits;
> we restore justice. Amen.

Fourth Sunday of Advent
2 SAMUEL 7:1-11,16
PSALM 89:1-4,19-26
ROMANS 16:25-27
LUKE 1:26-38

Promised One,
Holy One of Faith:
> the Arc of your Love
>> overshadows all creation;
> the touch of your Holiness
>> finds favor with all creatures;
> the power of your Deliverance
>> makes each child your own.

May we rejoice, with Mary,
for we are highly favored
to be servants of the Most High. Amen.

CHRISTMAS

FEAST OF THE NATIVITY
SEE YEAR A

CHRISTMAS EVE LATE
SEE YEAR A

FIRST SUNDAY AFTER CHRISTMAS
SEE YEAR A

SECOND SUNDAY AFTER CHRISTMAS
SEE YEAR A

EPIPHANY

FIRST SUNDAY AFTER EPIPHANY – BAPTISM OF JESUS
GENESIS 1:1-5
PSALM 29
ACTS 19:1-7
MARK 1:4-11

Creating God,
over the churning chaos of our lives
your Spirit ceaselessly broods:

> may our hearts become emptiness;
> may our souls be simple darkness;

so we, like Christ,
may hear your heavenly voice speaking
through the face of the Deep –

> "You are my Beloved, my Own.
> On You my favor rests." Amen.

Second Sunday after Epiphany

1 Samuel 3:1-10, (11-20)
Psalm 139:1-5,12-17
1 Corinthians 6:12-20
John 1:43-51

God of Daybreak,
your light dawns anew this morning
as the lamp of our soul:
> begotten of your Word
>> we are each God's Own;
> members of Christ's body
>> we are not dominated by anything;
> stitched together in your Spirit
>> we are drawn to come and see

that the glories of heaven are
manifest now as the gifts of creation. Amen.

Third Sunday after Epiphany

Jonah 3:1-5,10
Psalm 62:5-12
1 Corinthians 7:29-31
Mark 1:14-20

God of Daylight,
You break in upon our slumbering souls and bid us awake:

> your light disperses the shadows of despair,
>> teaching our hearts to trust;
> your light casts off the weight of worry,
>> showing our minds the way of hope;
> your light dispels the weakness in our bones,
>> rooting our lives in your strength.

NOW, is the time of fulfillment.
NOW, is your reign at hand.
NOW, do our souls follow
> and find rest in You alone. Amen.

Fourth Sunday after Epiphany
Deuteronomy 18:15-20
Psalm 111
1 Corinthians 8:1-13
Mark 1:21-28

Gracious God,
Beloved Sovereign of the universe,
your generous rule is the Word of Love:
> we would kill for the sake of transient thoughts of our minds,
>> but Christ's fire melts the false metal of our pride;
> we would hang others with our demeaning words,
>> but Christ's Presence uncoils the knot of our fear.

Be this day the Author of our hearts,
teaching us that there is no God but the One
who is Love released. Amen.

Fifth Sunday after Epiphany
Isaiah 40:21-31
Psalm 147:1-12,21c
1 Corinthians 9:16-23
Mark 1:29-39

Holy One,
Creator of the Universe:
your heavenly beauty lights the stars,
> and of stardust we are made;
your forgiving embrace stretches out like the skies,
> and we are a tent of faith that welcomes all;
your depth of understanding love is unsearchable,
> and we are at rest in your mystery.

May You be the power that stirs our souls to justice;
> so that in Christ,
>> we may run and not get weary,
>>> we may walk and never tire. Amen.

Sixth Sunday after Epiphany
2 Kings 5:1-14
Psalm 30
1 Corinthians 9:24-27
Mark 1:40-45

Most Merciful,
your favor endures forever,
your Presence renews our hearts.
In Christ we know that none are lost to You.
With Christ we return all creation to your care.
In Christ we know your will to heal.
With Christ we are a body of mercy for all.
May your anointing Spirit wash over and cleanse us this day,
releasing your divine favor as a flood of grace. Amen.

Last Sunday after Epiphany
2 Kings 2:1-12
Psalm 50:1-6
2 Corinthians 4:3-6
Mark 9:2-9

Transfiguring Flame,
your fiery Presence
burns away all falseness.
May our hearts, like that of Jesus your Beloved,
    be consumed with your compassion to renew all life.
May nothing but light shine forth from our souls
    consuming all traces of selfishness.
May we be transfigured through and through
    in the likeness of Christ our Lord. Amen.

LENT

ASH WEDNESDAY
SEE YEAR A

FIRST SUNDAY IN LENT
GENESIS 9:8-17
PSALM 25:1-9
1 PETER 3:18-22
MARK 1:9-15

God of the everlasting covenant,
your wild embracing love
compassionately cradles and surely strengthens
all for the journey:
> When we would become lost and imprisoned
> > in the small worlds of our own making.
> When we would become disoriented
> > by the wild beasts of our passions.

Steady our souls to enter the wilderness of our fears.
Teach us to discover the angels present within our frantic beasts.
Encourage us in the steady, strong, way of Love,
so that we arrive in You,
cradling creation as Christ . Amen.

SECOND SUNDAY IN LENT
GENESIS 17:1-7,15-16
PSALM 22:22-30
ROMANS 4:13-25
MARK 8:31-38

God of Sarah and Abraham,
You are the Mother and Father
of all creation:
> may we fall on our face
> > in your merciful presence;
> may we surrender our souls
> > receiving your Hope against hope;
> may we release all that our hearts clutch and
> > know your saving Presence which
> > restores the dead to life. Amen.

Third Sunday in Lent
EXODUS 20:1-17
PSALM 19
1 CORINTHIANS 1:18-25
JOHN 2:13-22

Holy God,
Holy and Mighty,
your words are sweeter than honey,
your wisdom refreshes the soul.
May we become fools for your love,
    with eyes to see your handiwork
    in the skies and throughout the earth.
May your Spirit drive the falseness from our souls
    that with Christ as our dwelling place,
        You gladden our hearts,
        and we bow to no one but You. Amen.

Fourth Sunday in Lent
NUMBERS 21:4-9
PSALM 107:1-3,17-22
EPHESIANS 2:1-10
JOHN 3:14-21

Holy God,
Holy and Merciful,
we are your divine work of art,
created in Christ Jesus.
Draw us away from our self-centered whims,
    bring us to life in Christ.
Teach us the folly of acting on every desire we have,
    return us to the wellspring of Christ.
Draw us forth from the dark shadows of fear and anger
    and lead us
        to dwell in the light of Christ, our life. Amen.

Fifth Sunday in Lent
Jeremiah 31:31-34
Psalm 51:1-13
Hebrews 5:5-10
John 12:20-33

Holy God,
Holy Immortal One,
You alone are God and
we are your people:
>your holy Law is upon our minds,
>>may we know not falseness;
>your holy Law is upon our hearts,
>>may we hunger for none but You.

Teach us to fall upon your earth
>and to die as nothing in your embrace.

Hear now our supplications with cries and tears,
>and bring from us a rich harvest in Christ Jesus. Amen.

Palm Sunday
Gathering – Liturgy of the Palms
Mark 11:1-11
Psalm 118:1-2, 19-29

Presider: Blessed is the King
>who comes in the name of the Lord.

Assembly: Peace in heaven and glory in the highest.

Presider: Let us pray together
Sovereign of creation,
You show us the path of life:
hungry neither for honor nor glory,
The Anointed One completely empties his heart;
deceived neither by flattery nor promise,
The Anointed One rests only in your presence.
Release us from the fear of being forsaken,
so that with the last breath
our soul cries out,
"My Lord and my God." Amen.

Maundy Thursday – Sent to Serve
See Year A for Collects and Page 149 for the Liturgy

Good Friday – The Cycle of Suffering Ceases
See Year A for Collects and Page 151 for the Liturgy

Easter Vigil
See page 156

EASTER

Easter Day – Life Renewed
Isaiah 25:6-9
Psalm 118:1-2,14-24
Acts 10:34-43
1 Corinthians 15:1-1
John 20:1-18

Presider: Alleluia. Christ is risen.
Assembly: **Christ is risen indeed. Alleluia.**
Presider: Alleluia. Christ is risen.
Assembly: **Christ is risen indeed. Alleluia.**
Presider: Alleluia. Christ is risen.
Assembly: **Christ is risen indeed. Alleluia.**
Presider: The Lord is with you.
Assembly: **And also with you.**
Presider: Let us pray together:
**Sun of Righteousness,
so gloriously risen,
shine in our hearts as we celebrate our redemption,
that we may see your way to our eternal home,
where You reign,
one holy and undivided Trinity,
now and for ever. Amen.**

Second Sunday of Easter

Acts 4:32-35
Psalm 133
1 John 1:1-2:2
John 20:19-31

Presider: Alleluia. Christ is risen.
Assembly: **Christ is risen indeed. Alleluia.**
Presider: Alleluia. Christ is risen.
Assembly: **Christ is risen indeed. Alleluia.**
Presider: Alleluia. Christ is risen.
Assembly: **Christ is risen indeed. Alleluia.**
Presider: The Lord is with you.
Assembly: **And also with you.**
Presider: Let us pray together:
**Our Savior and our God,
You alone are the Word
who is Life.
In your Word we are one with Christ,
    all children of the Spirit.
Through your Word darkness fades,
    our souls radiant of Easter light.
With your Word as the voice of our hearts,
    purifying us from all blind falsehood,
    we cry out with our brother Thomas,
my Savior and my God. Amen.**

Third Sunday of Easter

ACTS 3:12-19
PSALM 4
1 JOHN 3:1-7
LUKE 24:36B-48

Presider: Alleluia. Christ is risen.
Assembly: **Christ is risen indeed. Alleluia.**
Presider: Alleluia. Christ is risen.
Assembly: **Christ is risen indeed. Alleluia.**
Presider: Alleluia. Christ is risen.
Assembly: **Christ is risen indeed. Alleluia.**
Presider: The Lord is with you.
Assembly: **And also with you.**
Presider: Let us pray together:
**Holy and Just One,
Author of Life:
    fill our mind so fully
        that we know nothing but You;
    claim our heart so completely
        that we desire nothing but You;
    permeate our body so thoroughly
        that we sense nothing but You;
At last, when our souls are at rest in You,
    we will be like God.
Transfigured through and through,
no trace of remainder,
a Resurrection people. Amen.**

Fourth Sunday of Easter
Acts 4:5-12
Psalm 23
1 John 3:16-24
John 10:11-18

Presider: Alleluia. Christ is risen.
Assembly: **Christ is risen indeed. Alleluia.**
Presider: Alleluia. Christ is risen.
Assembly: **Christ is risen indeed. Alleluia.**
Presider: Alleluia. Christ is risen.
Assembly: **Christ is risen indeed. Alleluia.**
Presider: The Lord is with you.
Assembly: **And also with you.**
Presider: Let us pray together:
**Jesus Christ, the Good Shepherd,
Our body was Your clothing,
Your Spirit was our Robe.
Robed in the eternal glory of Love,
   may we know the Resurrection courage
   to lay down our lives.
Robed in the eternal glory of Love,
   may we know the Resurrection truth that
   God became human so that we might become god.
Robed in the eternal glory of Love,
   good shepherds all,
   may we fear no danger,
   as we commit our lives
   to the salvation of God's Paradise. Amen.**

inspired by St. Ephrem the Syrian

Fifth Sunday of Easter

Acts 8:26-40
Psalm 22:24-30
1 John 4:7-21
John 15:1-8

Presider: Alleluia. Christ is risen.
Assembly: **Christ is risen indeed. Alleluia.**
Presider: Alleluia. Christ is risen.
Assembly: **Christ is risen indeed. Alleluia.**
Presider: Alleluia. Christ is risen.
Assembly: **Christ is risen indeed. Alleluia.**
Presider: The Lord is with you.
Assembly: **And also with you.**
Presider: Let us pray together:
Holy Love,
You are the tender and tenacious Mother Vine.
All life flows from your Love –
    for none may cut off the reach of your bounty.
All knowledge flows from your Love–
    for Wisdom alone satisfies the heart.
All perfection flows from your Love –
    for in You we are without blemish.
Mother Christ,
Source and Sustenance of all,
we arise as your sweet fruit,
in whom the world tastes
    no fear, no hate, no blindness –
only You. Amen.

Sixth Sunday of Easter

ACTS 10:44-48
PSALM 98
1 JOHN 5:1-6
JOHN 15:9-17

Presider: Alleluia. Christ is risen.
Assembly: **Christ is risen indeed. Alleluia.**
Presider: Alleluia. Christ is risen.
Assembly: **Christ is risen indeed. Alleluia.**
Presider: Alleluia. Christ is risen.
Assembly: **Christ is risen indeed. Alleluia.**
Presider: The Lord is with you.
Assembly: **And also with you.**
Presider: Let us pray together:
**Beloved Song of Life,
as rivers clap their hands and
hills ring for joy,
our own hearts break forth into a chorus of praise:
    blessed be the Beloved,
        whose justice is the tender touch of forgiveness;
    blessed be the Beloved,
        whose salvation is the sweet surrender of friendship;
    blessed be the Beloved,
        whose commandment is the gift of love.
Whatever You ask of us this day, Dear One,
we offer to You in the joy of Christ's love. Amen.**

Seventh Sunday of Easter
Acts 1:15-17, 21-26
Psalm 1
1 John 5:9-13
John 17:6-19

Presider: Alleluia. Christ is risen.
Assembly: **Christ is risen indeed. Alleluia.**
Presider: Alleluia. Christ is risen.
Assembly: **Christ is risen indeed. Alleluia.**
Presider: Alleluia. Christ is risen.
Assembly: **Christ is risen indeed. Alleluia.**
Presider: The Lord is with you.
Assembly: **And also with you.**
Presider: Let us pray together:
**Holy One of Blessing,
in You we are like strong cedars
planted by flowing water,
drawing forth Life from the current of Love
to bear the fruit of Peace:
   Peace that flows from belonging to You;
   Peace that flows from being one with You;
   Peace that flows from being of You alone.
Consecrate us to your Heart this day,
so that as You read our hearts
they speak only of your Presence. Amen.**

Pentecost

Feast of Pentecost
Acts 2:1-21
Psalm 104:25-35,37
Romans 8:22-27
John 15:26-27;16:4b-15

Breath of Life,
You enfold the vast deep
and all creation springs forth from You
with the fire of life.
    Breathe in us the Spirit of Hope –
        that our hearts might groan beyond the grasp of words,
        grateful for our birth in You.
    Breathe in us the Spirit of Salvation –
        that our souls might cry out in sweet thanksgiving,
        for in You we are set free from all fear.
    Breathe in us the Spirit of Fire –
        that our bodies might be drunk with your burning Presence,
        for as You rest upon us and all creation,
        we awaken to the Truth we thirst to know:
        we belong to Love alone. Amen.

Trinity Sunday
Isaiah 6:1-8
Psalm 29
Romans 8_12-17
John 3:1-17

Beloved Giver of Life,
all we are
we receive with grateful hearts.
You alone are the Source of life,
    for all that lives is born of You.
You alone are the Word of life,
    for You speak and all comes forth.
You alone are the Breath of life,
    for when You sing
the delightful dance of all creation unfolds.
May the dance be our gift to you,
life freely spun from the Giver of Life. Amen.

PROPER 6
EZEKIEL 17:22-24
PSALM 20
2 CORINTHIANS 5:6-10,(11-13),14-17
MARK 4:26-34

Faithful God,
Beloved One,
in the shelter of your divine Heart
is strengthening shade for our journey.
Traveling as one,
You teach us through the Word of parables
to place the trust of hearts in the Beloved alone:

You sow the seed of Faith as the very soil of our soul;
You plant your holy kiss with abandon upon our searching hearts;
You continually draw us forward in a pilgrim journey of love.

May our lives unfold as tender yet strong green shoots –
receiving all in your name and returning all in your trust. Amen.

PROPER 7
JOB 38:1-11
PSALM 107:1-3,23-32
2 CORINTHIANS 6:1-13
MARK 4:35-41

God of Abraham, Sarah, and Hagar,
when we are flung to sky and then plunged to the depths,
> You are faithful.

God of Moses and Miriam,
when we are stunned and staggered by life's sorrows,
> You are faithful.

God of Naomi and Ruth,
when courage fails and we clutch close what we've known,
> You are faithful.

God of Mary Magdalene and Mark,
when gales of passion arise and break in upon our lives;
when in fright we would close our hearts and lower our eyes:
> You bid us to believe that now is the acceptable time;
> You are the quiet calm within our souls
>> inviting us to cross over to the other shore
>> and know again
>> that You are faithful. Amen.

Proper 8

Wisdom of Solomon 1:13-15;2:23-24
Lamentations 3:21-33
(or) Psalm 30
2 Corinthians 8:7-15
Mark 5:21-43

Praise God's holy name,
> we are created to be imperishable.

Praise God's holy name,
> we are images of the divine face.

Praise God's holy name,
> The Beloved's favor endures forever.

Praise God's holy name,
> The Beloved created all things to be alive.

Praise God's holy name,
> The Beloved changes our despair into dance. Amen.

Proper 9

Ezekiel 2:1-5
Psalm 123
2 Corinthians 12:2-10
Mark 6:1-13

Beloved Sovereign,
You are enthroned in our hearts
as the gracious seat of eternal Mercy:
> we lift our eyes to you,
>> strengthened in your sweet and sure compassion;
> we open our ears to you,
>> listening for your thundering Word of silent and certain hope;
> we stand up humbly before you,
>> mortal and divine, broken and beautiful.

May the quickening of your holy Spirit
> shake off the complacent dust binding our souls,
> thrusting open hearts of mercy
> that receive each as your anointed one. Amen.

Proper 10
Amos 7:7-15
Psalm 85:8-13
Ephesians 1:3-14
Mark 6:14-29

Beloved and Faithful One:
  the only measure of your Heart is forgiveness-
    may we stand humbly before you;
  the stilling sound of your Voice is shalom-
    may we speak peaceful words of justice;
  the certain touch of your Hand is the royal sanctuary of creation-
    may we lean down and care for your creatures.
Remembering that in Christ all are chosen,
may the land of our soul yield the Spirit's harvest
of goodness, praise, and thanksgiving. Amen.

Proper 11
Jeremiah 23:1-6
Psalm 23
Ephesians 2:11-22
Mark 6:30-34,53-56

Beloved Shepherd,
our souls are your very pasture
anointed as the presence of Christ:
        even if we feel surrounded by the shadows of death;
        even if we feel lost and without direction;
        even if we feel tired with coming and going;
You are with us –
        the rod of your Holy Truth, our strength;
        the staff of your Holy Faith, our courage.
May we be shepherds of your justice,
restoring Holy Hope for days without end. Amen.

Proper 12
2 Kings 4:42-44
Psalm 145:10-19
Ephesians 3:14-21
John 6:1-21

Beloved,
your power now at work in us
does immeasurably more than we can ask or imagine.
Instruct us in the ways of Holy Wisdom:
    teach us to cease our wandering and to sit down,
        for Christ dwells in our trusting hearts;
    teach us to release our fear and walk upon life's waters,
        for we are rooted and grounded in the Ark of love;
    teach us that your Presence alone
        satisfies the desire of every living thing. Amen.

Proper 13
Exodus 16:2-4,9-15
Psalm 78:23-29
Ephesians 4:1-16
John 6:24-35

Beloved Companion,
in the Chosen One is the bread of life:

    empty of pride, Jesus humbly receives You;
    empty of anger, Jesus serenely embodies You;
    empty of all plans, Jesus in constancy hears You.

Fed on the emptiness of Jesus,
may the Spirit teach us that we also are chosen
to be empty of our selves and
filled only with your Life. Amen.

Proper 14
1 Kings 19:4-8
Psalm 34:1-8
Ephesians 4:25-5:2
John 6:35,41-51

Tender One,
in the Chosen One is the bread of life.
May the bread of life strengthen our souls
for the journey of transfiguration:

> transforming rage and anger into love and peace,
> transforming slander and malice into truth and compassion,
> transforming judgment into mutual forgiveness.

Show us how to walk in love as Christ loves us,
being fragrant gifts of the Spirit. Amen.

Proper 15
Proverbs 9:1-6
Psalm 34:9-14
Ephesians 5:15-20
John 6:51-58

Holy Wisdom:
> Foolishly we wonder where you dwell,
> > yet you build us as your very house.
> Foolishly we wander about in the shadows of our passions,
> > yet your warm light shines from the hearth of our hearts.
> Foolishly we hunger as we feast upon the fool's gold of
> acceptance,
> > yet the Bread of Life, who satisfies,
> > is already deep within.

Enlighten our souls, Holy Wisdom,
that we may become pilgrims
of our own holy ground. Amen.

PROPER 16
JOSHUA 24:1-2A,14-18
PSALM 34:15-22
EPHESIANS 6:10-20
JOHN 6:56-69

Beloved,
not one of us can come to Love
unless we awake from our slumber.
May Love transform the passionate powers
that dominate our lives
and teach us the path of saving Wisdom:

> when our hearts are broken,
> > You are close;
> when our minds are troubled,
> > You deliver;
> when our bodies are broken,
> > You protect.

Restore our souls, O Love,
that we might completely and sincerely
revere and serve You. Amen.

PROPER 17
DEUTERONOMY 4:1-2,6-9
PSALM 15
JAMES 1:17-27
MARK 7:1-8,14-15,21-23

God of our Ancestors,
we search for You in desert and on mountain top.
We are driven by hungry hearts,
> batted about by greed, deceit, and envy.
We are frozen by anxious minds,
> captured by the fear of failure.
Remind our hearts that deep, deep, within,
> You have planted your Law,
> your Love, your Life.
May we truly be your beloved tent,
> the holy mountain in whom You dwell. Amen.

PROPER 18
ISAIAH 35:4-7A
PSALM 146
JAMES 2:1-10,(11-13),14-17
MARK 7:24-37

Faithful God,
in your Heart alone lives Hope.
When our eyes are blinded by hate,
    Christ opens our hearts to beauty.
When our ears are deafened by judgment,
    Christ unseals our hearts to truth.
When our limbs are paralyzed by fear,
    Christ loosens our hearts to the salvation of touch.
Creation is a chorus of your sweet goodness.
May your Wisdom teach our hearts to hear and receive You
and turn our speech into the anthem of praise:
the Beloved does *everything* well! Amen.

PROPER 19
ISAIAH 50:4-9A
PSALM 116:1-8
JAMES 3:1-12
MARK 8:27-38

Exalted God,
morning after morning You awaken creation
and await the song of thanksgiving and praise.
Who do we say that You are?
    You are Compassion, curing the hunger of our hearts.
Who do we say that You are?
    You are Wisdom, showing the path of life through death.
Who do we say that You are?
    You are the Holy Source of life on fire –
    Praise be our God and Creator. Amen.

Proper 20

WISDOM OF SOLOMON 1:16-2:1,12-22
PSALM 54
JAMES 3:13-4:3,7-8A
MARK 9:30-37

Holy Wisdom,
You search the corners of our souls,
weary from the conflicts and battles of our hearts,
for traces of Life, sparks of Light, and vestiges of Love.

Though we continually indulge our own pleasures,
our deep longing
       is to become as vulnerable and innocent as children.

Though the hunger of ambition fuels our wearisome restlessness,
our true hope
       lies in our repose within You.

Though self-pride drives the conceit of our own small minds,
our salvation
       comes from humble hospitality to all in your name.

Still the ceaseless and fruitless arguments of our hearts,
       that our souls may find life and light and love
              in Christ, our Holy Wisdom. Amen.

Proper 21
Numbers 11:4-6,10-16,24-29
Psalm 19:7-14
James 5:13-20
Mark 9:38-50

Beloved,
Holy Origin and Divine Source of life:
    when our hearts wail in desire for what is past;
    when our hearts ache with longing for what might be;
    when our hearts cry out in jealousy, "stop"!;
    when our hearts complain with the conviction
        that you are absent —

Transform this anxious envy.
Return the gaze of our souls deep within,
where Wisdom reigns
and reveals that the kiss of Christ alone bears all life into being —
    each creature is a word of the Word,
    each word is Holy,
    and creation is a chorus of Wisdom for the way. Amen.

inspired by Meister Eckhart

Proper 22
Genesis 2:18-24
Psalm 8
Hebrews 1:1-4;2:5-12
Mark 10:2-16

Beloved Friend,
your moist lips press against ours and breathe life —
    quickening these earthen vessels
    which you have made barely less than God.
Remind us this day,
lest we become lost
amidst the multitude and feel separate and alone,
that although we appear to be many,
we are one in You and each other —
    bone of your bone
    flesh of your flesh
    heart of your heart
    mind of your mind.
May our souls sing out with grateful praise
the sweet truth of your Name —
    we live *only* as One. Amen.

Proper 23

Amos 5:6-7,10-15
Psalm 90:12-17
Hebrews 4:12-16
Mark 10:17-31

Good Teacher,
unveil for us the saving Wisdom of Christ.
May your Word pierce so deeply
that it divides bone from marrow,
baring our tender heart before your healing eyes.
Possess our souls from the inside out,
and show us the power of innocence,
so what was once impossible becomes our way of life:
Now,
> we love the good,
> we unmask the evil,
> we forgive the persecutor —
> we celebrate tender justice. Amen.

Proper 24

Isaiah 53:4-12
Psalm 91:9-16
Hebrews 5:1-10
Mark 10:35-45

Source of Life,
to each creature You confide,
> you are my own;
> today I have begotten you.

Word of Life,
remind us that
> You are rescue certain before all hate.
> You are refuge firm before all wrath.

Breath of Life,
when the world would accuse and destroy
your very own in the name of god;
may we stand with your begotten,
anointed with your Spirit,
lest a single limb be bruised. Amen.

Proper 25
JEREMIAH 31:7-9
PSALM 126
HEBREWS 7:23-28
MARK 10:46-52

Compassionate One,
like Bartimaeus, we forget who we are –
your Body, your Presence.

> We stumble blind in the dark
> shouting out, have pity on me.

> We feel captive and parched with loneliness
> crying out to become like streams in the driest desert.

> We wander vainly to the ends of the earth
> seeking only to be gathered in by you.

Yet our souls remember and beg for the wholeness
You have already graciously given.
Remind our hearts once more of your joyous Presence,
and be the Light guiding our journey home. Amen.

All Saints
WISDOM OF SOLOMON 2:1-9
PSALM 24
REVELATION 21:1-6A
JOHN 11:32-44

Holy Wisdom,
> so often we stand paralyzed and entombed within despair,
> dreading that life is but a passing shadow.

Holy Wisdom,
> so often we ask, where *do* you reside?
> Where *is* your holy place?
> Where *are* the doors that we might enter?

Holy Wisdom
> so often we ask
> whether the fleeting sweet pleasures of the senses
> are all that remain to us?

Our hearts cry "no,"
> for they are your Tabernacle and know the Truth.

Holy Wisdom
> we hear your voice –
>> God alone is the Alpha and Omega,
>> the endless ocean
>> in Whom we live, we die, we are. Amen.

Proper 26
RUTH 1:1-18
PSALM 146
HEBREWS 9:11-14
MARK 12:28-34

Listen, Beloved, to the cry of your lover:
    Do not spurn me and leave me cold.
    Do not find a home apart from my heart.
    Do not look past me for the face of another.
Where You go,
        I will go.
We are One,
    as You are One.
Press upon me,
    Beloved,
        until *we* breathe no more:
            Christ's Heart *become* mine –
                and I am no more:
                      the kingdom of God come. Amen.

Proper 27
1 KINGS 17:8-16
PSALM 146
HEBREWS 9:24-28
MARK 12:38-44

God of Infinite Generosity,
        in the offering of the poor widow
        is manifest the selfless love of Christ.
Our heart would seek from others in vain
        what they simply cannot provide:
            respect,
            freedom,
            peace.
Turn the eyes of our heart upon you, deep within.
Soften our soul that we might release all we possess
        and all we are.
Transform our hunger for honor into Holy Hope –
            where we become nothing but Christ's love,
            sustenance for a starving world. Amen.

Proper 28
Daniel 12:1-3
Psalm 16
Hebrews 10:11-14,(15-18),19-25
Mark 13:1-8

Faithful Beloved,
Your Spirit is the midwife of life:
> In Christ, the darkness of control gives way
>> to the light of courage.
> In Christ, the shadows of shame
>> dissolve into souls of serenity.
> In Christ, we are no longer strangers to ourselves –
>> false facades are torn down,
>> the great exile is past.

May we live in Christ, with the Beloved our only food and drink.
May we become the city of God
> with God alone all that we have. Amen.

Last Sunday after Pentecost – Christ the King
Daniel 7:9-10,13-14
Psalm 93
Revelation 1:4b-8
John 18:33-37

Ancient of Days,
in Christ is made known
that self-emptying is the decisive authority of the universe.

> Your Realm is in this world but not of this world –
>> holy power is Innocence.
> Your Presence is in this world but not of this world –
>> divine law is Mercy.

Release us, like Jesus,
> from the tyrannical rule of our ego's desire.
May our empty hearts burn bright with boundless compassion,
> receiving whoever stands before us
> as your holy Presence –
> the Alpha and Omega of life. Amen.

Year C
Advent

First Sunday of Advent
Jeremiah 33:14-16
Psalm 25:1-9
1 Thessalonians 3:9-13
Luke 21:25-36

Beloved Creator,
a voice, your voice, cries out to us on the wind,
bidding us return to the land of our soul:

Worldly cares consume us then depart on the wind,
    yet Justice grows strong and sure in the land of our soul.

Fear freezes us fast and then surely fades,
    while the Heart grows strong and sure in the land of our soul.

Heaven and earth are *now* passing away,
    as the Word grows strong and sure in the land of our soul.

Christ is the hallowed ground of our own divine planting,
and so Hope is the harvest in the land of our soul. Amen.

Second Sunday of Advent
Baruch 5:1-9
Canticle 16
Philippians 1:3-11
Luke 3:1-6

Beloved Creator,
a voice, your voice, cries out to us on the wind,
revealing that all life is one ocean of grace,
the continually unfolding Christ:

Every valley carved cold with the steel of hatred
    is filled wondrously by the touch of compassion.
Every mountain built from the sediment of fear
    is leveled by the courage to clear a straight road.
All the twisted paths hewn by the works of our hands,
    the dreams of our minds,
    and the desires of our hearts,
    are made straight and smooth
    by the all-accomplishing wisdom of Love.

May the waters of Christ nourish a trust so deep and clear
that the eyes of our souls
see only a gracious and harmonious unfoldment
of your Love. Amen.

Third Sunday of Advent

ZEPHANIAH 3:14-20
CANTICLE 9
PHILIPPIANS 4:4-7
LUKE 3:7-18

Beloved Creator,
a voice, your voice, cries out to us on the wind,
bringing forth a cry of wild joy from our hearts:

> In Jesus, we see the Wisdom of God
> bearing no wrath, but forgiveness alone.
>
> In Jesus, we see the Mercy of God
> winnowing away our ignorance, fear, anger and deceit.
>
> In Jesus, we see the unquenchable fire of Divine Love
> burning clean the land of our soul.

Jesus is the Divine mirror
placed before the eyes of hearts:
Rejoice, as we behold the birth of Christ. Amen.

Fourth Sunday of Advent
Micah 5:2-5a
Canticle 15
Hebrews 10:5-10
Luke 1:39-45,(46-55)

Beloved Creator,
a voice, your voice, cries out to us on the wind,
releasing our once cautious and careful hearts
to dance and leap with joyous abandon:

Our souls proclaim your greatness, O God,
    for the strength of your arm scatters the conceit of our pride.

Our spirits rejoice in You, O Savior,
    for You depose our egos from their thrones of might.

Our blessed bodies cry out that holy is your Name,
    for You empty our lives of cluttered false riches
    and prepare the wombs of our hearts
    for the birth of Christ. Amen.

Christmas

Feast of the Nativity
See Year A

Christmas Eve Late
See Year A

First Sunday after Christmas
See Year A

Second Sunday after Christmas
See Year A

Epiphany

First Sunday after Epiphany – Baptism of Jesus

Isaiah 43:1-7
Psalm 29
Acts 8:14-17
Luke 3:15-17, 21-22

Spirit of Leah and Rachel and Jacob,
Spirit of Jesus, the Beloved:
    create us,
    fashion us,
    and redeem us.
Spirit hovering over the deep of our souls:
Lead us into the midst of the Holy Fire,
    that your flames might forge courageous hearts
    tempered through love of You.
Draw us ever deeper into the Divine Sea,
    that we may we fully die,
    yet not drown,
    in the waters of baptism. Amen.

~OR

Beloved,
our hearts long to know
the awesome beauty of your face flush upon ours.
Be unto us the Strength
    that carries us up the mountain.
Be unto us the Grace
    that lifts the veil of our ignorance and fear.
Awaken us to the great and abiding Truth:
    each child is called to become radiant
        -- transformed and transfigured --
            like Jesus Christ,
so that your Spirit rejoices,
    This is my Own, my Chosen One. Listen. Amen.

SECOND SUNDAY AFTER EPIPHANY
ISAIAH 62:1-5
PSALM 36:5-10
1 CORINTHIANS 12:1-11
JOHN 2:1-11

Dear and sweet Beloved,
our hearts are delirious
from drinking deeply of the wine of the Spirit.
Christ arises within Jerusalem like the nuptial moon,
    whispering softly in our ears, "you are My Delight."
Christ's holy lips meet ours,
    Lover to loved, in marriage's delight.
Christ crowns our countenance with a garland of beauty,
    and our thirst for justice
        becomes the lover's delight. Amen.

THIRD SUNDAY AFTER EPIPHANY
NEHEMIAH 8:1-3,5-6,8-10
PSALM 19
1 CORINTHIANS 12:12-31A
LUKE 4:14-21

Let us bless God, the Most High,
who is the joy of our heart
and the strength of our soul.

Let us bless God, the Most High,
whose Presence is sweeter than honey upon the tongue,
and whose embrace gladdens our heart.

Let us bless God, the Most High,
whose Spirit is a tender kiss upon Jesus and all creatures,
anointing great and small.

Let us bless God, the Most High,
for creation is one precious and delicate body,
and God's favor rests with us all. Amen.

Fourth Sunday after Epiphany
Jeremiah 1:4-10
Psalm 71:1-17
1 Corinthians 13:1-13
Luke 4:21-30

Holy One,
may the starlight embers of your Spirit
rekindle our soul's longing
to be Christ's love in the world:

Love is a solid mountain of strength,
  gathering all in like the resolute arms of a father.
Love is the sure kiss of forgiveness,
  reassuring broken hearts of the Beloved's presence.
Love is a vast reservoir of hope,
  reminding fearful and narrow minds
  to relax and trust.
Love is the very marrow of Divine Justice,
  enduring,
    as all else resolves into dust.

We are Love, or we are not at all. Amen.

Last Sunday after Epiphany
Exodus 34:29-35
Psalm 99
2 Corinthians 3:12-4:2
Luke 9:28-36(37-43)

Holy, Holy, Holy God,
You alone
are unfathomable and eternal Love.
Love cries out to us from the deep:
 "Come, pull out and away
  from the safe shore to which you cling so desperately.
   Leave your home – it is empty.
   Desert your city – its promises waste your time.
   Let go of false treasures – they only enslave."
May our hearts drop deep, deep, endlessly deep,
 into the emptiness of Christ.
   Then may we know
    the dark richness of life
filled with God's spacious glory. Amen.

LENT

ASH WEDNESDAY
SEE YEAR A

FIRST SUNDAY IN LENT
DEUTERONOMY 26:1-11
PSALM 91:1-2, 9-16
ROMANS 10:8B-13
LUKE 4:1-13

Sovereign of my heart,
Beloved of my soul –
fertile Ground of life,
your Spirit cries out to your famished ones:
    "return to the land of your soul,
    a land flowing with milk and honey.
    When you would hunger for bread,
        remember that I alone fill the soul.
    When you would be prostrate before power and glory,
        remember that I alone satisfy the soul.
    When you would reject life's sorrow
    and seek me only in safety and security,
        remember that the land of your soul
        is the Ground Christ tread.
    Return to the land of your soul,
        for you are the body of Christ." Amen.

SECOND SUNDAY IN LENT
GENESIS 15:1-12,17-18
PSALM 27
PHILIPPIANS 3:17-4:1
LUKE 13:31-35

Sovereign of my heart,
Beloved of my soul —
You say to my heart, "Seek my face."
More precious than life
      is the beauty of your countenance.
More dear than friends
      is the knowledge of your goodness.
One thing I seek.
One thing I know:
      your Presence is my house,
      my soul *is* your Presence. Amen.

THIRD SUNDAY IN LENT
EXODUS 3:1-15
PSALM 63:1-8
1 CORINTHIANS 10:1-13
LUKE 13:1-9

Sovereign of my heart,
Beloved of my soul —
You are the deep and the shallow.
You are the fertile as well as the fallow.
You are the honey and the bitter.
You are the fire as well as the winter.
You are the center and the edge,
      -- and, in Truth, all between.
You are I Am,
      and I am, too.
I am your shadow,
      and my soul clings to you. Amen.

Fourth Sunday in Lent
Joshua 5:9-12
Psalm 32
2 Corinthians 5:16-21
Luke 15:1-3, 11b-32

Sovereign of my heart,
Beloved of my soul —
like a father
who beholds his confused child
only through a heart-in-love,
your eyes embrace us whole.
When we would shrink away beneath needless shame,
  your robe of finest mercy resurrects our soul.
When petty anger would fuel our refusal to receive,
  your love is steadfast and withholds nothing.
Throw your arms about us this day
  and kiss sweetly our hearts. Amen.

Fifth Sunday in Lent
Isaiah 43:16-21
Psalm 126
Philippians 3:4b-14
John 12:1-8

Sovereign of my heart,
Beloved of my soul —
your Heart cries out from the depths of the sea:
  "memory traps you in the wasteland —
    forget the past;
  planning ensnares you in the wasteland —
    forget the future.
 Now,
   this very moment,
    water springs forth from your heart.
    Can't you see it?
 Forsake all for Christ,
  and your captive heart flows free." Amen.

Palm Sunday
Gathering – Liturgy of the Palms
LUKE 19:28-40
PSALM 118:1-2, 19-29

Presider: Blessed is the King
 who comes in the name of the Lord.
Assembly: Peace in heaven and glory in the highest.
Presider: Let us pray together
Sovereign of creation,
You show us the path of life:
hungry neither for honor nor glory,
The Anointed One completely empties his heart;
deceived neither by flattery nor promise,
The Anointed One's path arises from your Presence.
Release us from the fear of being forsaken,
so that with the last breath
our soul cries out,
"my Lord and my God." Amen.

Maundy Thursday – Sent to Serve
SEE YEAR A FOR COLLECTS AND PAGE 149 FOR THE LITURGY

Good Friday – The Cycle of Suffering Ceases
SEE YEAR A FOR COLLECTS AND PAGE 151 FOR THE LITURGY

Easter Vigil
SEE PAGE 156

EASTER

EASTER SUNDAY – LIFE RENEWED
ISAIAH 65.17-25
PSALM 118.1-2,14-24
ACTS 10: 34-43
MATTHEW 24.1-12

Presider: There is one Body and one Spirit;
Assembly: **There is one hope in God's call to us;**
Presider: One Lord, one Faith, one Baptism;
Assembly: **One God and Father of all.**
Presider: The Lord is with you.
Assembly: **And also with you.**
Presider: Let us pray together
**In water are we conceived.
In water are we knit together in the Spirit.
Through the breaking of water are we born.
Through the drinking of water are we nourished.
You, O God,** *are* **the living water:
    wash over us, again and again and again,
that in Christ we might live as
    your daughters and sons,
and that with Christ as our heart
we might respect the dignity of every human being. Amen.**

SECOND SUNDAY OF EASTER
ACTS 5:27-32
PSALM 118:14-29
REVELATION 1:4-8
JOHN 20:19-31

Beloved,
You are the Alpha and the Omega,
the very arc of divine love
coursing thru creation.
Cleanse the eyes of our hearts
so that we might behold as Christ
those whose pains and sorrows
we touch this day.
In the end, as in the beginning,
may the love we bare
be the very peace of God. **Amen.**

Third Sunday of Easter
Acts 9:1-6,(7-20)
Psalm 30
Revelation 5:11-14
John 21:1-19

Beloved,
be Thou our heart's courage
drawing us forth into the water.
Wash the scales from our eyes,
so that we might see who we truly are:
    followers of the Way –
        companions of those who suffer;
    followers of the Way –
        food for those who hunger.
May we *become* the Way we follow,
    the body of Christ offered for all. Amen.

Fourth Sunday of Easter
Acts 9:36-43
Psalm 23
Revelation 7:9-17
John 10:22-30

Beloved,
with You as the shepherd of our heart
we are never lost.
When we would be led astray and broken
    by the voices of want,
        You wipe away every last tear.
When we would feel tested and tried
    by our many fears,
        You carry us from death into life.
May our heart's own longing be your voice,
and may we know Love unfailing
    to be our heart. Amen.

Fifth Sunday of Easter
Acts 11:1-18
Psalm 148
Revelation 21:1-6
John 13:31-35

Alleluia!
Praise Mother God
        whose passionate loving
        conceives all creatures.
Look, in Jesus Love is making all things new:
        every living thing is clean in God's pure Love.
Loving one another is the Wisdom way,
        the only way,
                to praise our God. Amen.

Sixth Sunday of Easter
Acts 16:9-15
Psalm 67
Revelation 21:10,22-22:5
John 14:23-29

Beloved,
    your face forever smiles upon us.
Your kind Word
        shapes our hearts
                into your dwelling place.
Your sweet Breath
        fills our souls with life-giving water,
                clear as crystal.
May our lives be lived true to your Word,
        gentle, yet bold, acts of love,
                for all who thirst. Amen.

Ascension
Acts 1:1-11
Psalm 47
Psalm 93
Ephesians 1:15-23
Luke 24:44-53

Beloved God,
>in your Spirit we are eternally created;
>in your Spirit we are eternally transformed;
>in your Spirit we are eternally received in your heart
>>- with Christ,
>who lives and loves with you,
>now and forever. Amen.

Seventh Sunday of Easter
Acts 16:16-34
Psalm 97
Revelation 22:12-14,16-17,20-21
John 17:20-26

Beloved God,
your Spirit
ceaselessly creates
every living creature.
Be the Wisdom of our hearts,
leading us to know that
Christ is all in all,
now and forever more. Amen.

PENTECOST

DAY OF PENTECOST
GENESIS 11:1-9
OR ACTS 2:1-21
PSALM 104:25-35,37B
ROMANS 8:14-17
JOHN 14:8-17,(25-27)

Breath of God,
sweet Spirit of life:
    your shadow embraces the deep
        and life is born;
    your kiss presses the earth
        and humanity arises;
    your breath alone
        is our life, our help, and our way.
The only truth that matters
    is that we are one with You in Christ.
We bow in deepest gratitude,
    our lungs exclaiming –
        Alleluia! Alleluia! Alleluia!

TRINITY SUNDAY: FIRST SUNDAY AFTER PENTECOST
PROVERBS 8:1-4,22-31
PSALM 8
ROMANS 5:1-5
JOHN 16:12-15

Holy Wisdom,
You weave together,
and are the woven heart,
of every living being.
You are the Source of Life
    calling out from the deep.
You are the Word of Life
    giving birth to us all.
You are the Breath of Life
    dancing with delight
        amidst the work of your graceful hands.
We are yours, body and soul,
    and we place the trust of our heart in You. Amen.

PROPER 5
1 KINGS 17:8-16,(17-24)
PSALM 146
GALATIANS 1:11-24
LUKE 7:11-17

Tender God,
    be the Breath
    reviving my soul
    when judgment would bury me for dead
    beneath despair.
Carry my heart,
    like a child cradled fast in mother Christ's arms,
    returning me from the shadows
    into the warm light of your love. Amen.

PROPER 6
1 KINGS 21:1-10,[11-14],15-21A
PSALM 5:1-8
GALATIANS 2:15-21
LUKE 7:36-8:3

Beloved,
teach us to break open
our hearts –
    that we might anoint with tears of love
    that we might receive with kisses of gladness
those who stand before us.
For they are your anointed ones,
the body of Christ,
held in reverence and awe. Amen.

Proper 7
1 Kings 19:1-4,(5-7),8-15a
Psalm 42 & 43
Galatians 3:23-29
Luke 8:26-39

Holy Friend,
we stand here waiting,
with our whole being longing for You.
Our heart cries, where is our God?
Draw near to us
    as the quiet breeze within life's whirlwind;
    as the sure ground within our shifting worlds.
Your unfailing power is endless mercy –
    the gentle whisper of Christ the Beloved,
    still and certain,
    beating as our heart. Amen.

Proper 8
2 Kings 2:1-2,6-14
Psalm 77:1-2,11-20
Galatians 5:1,13-25
Luke 9:51-62

Praise the Beloved:
    as Christ is free, so are we.
Praise the Beloved:
    as Christ is love, so are we.
Praise the Beloved:
    as Christ is beautiful, so are we.
Praise the Beloved:
    as Christ lives, so do we. Amen.

Proper 9
2 Kings 5:1-14
Psalm 30
Galatians 6:(1-6),7-16
Luke 10:1-11,16-20

O Thou from whom comes the Breath of life:
    let *your* desire be
        the Wind washing through us,
        cleansing the desires of our hearts;
    let *your* counsel be
        the Wisdom restoring peace in our house,
        creating us anew as the likeness of Christ,
    the Breath of life. Amen.

inspired by Saadi Neil Douglas-Klotz's
transliteration of the Aramaic Lord's Prayer.

Proper 10
Amos 7:7-17
Psalm 82
Colossians 1:1-14
Luke 10:25-37

Tender God,
your divine Wind
births creation,
and You alone are life's inheritance.
Scatter the conceit of proud hearts,
    that your Love might guide our strength
    in the service of those broken by life.
Restore your Wisdom within us,
    that we, like Christ,
    might recognize and receive
    all we meet
    as your own holy of holies. Amen.

Proper 11
Amos 8:1-12
Psalm 52
Colossians 1:15-28
Luke 10:38-42

O Thou, Beloved,
the time is ripe beyond telling
for the mending touch of Christ upon our fractured lives.
>In Christ, the crushing rod of vengeance
>>is replaced by the Spirit of eternal forgiveness.
>In Christ, the famine of God's word
>>becomes a banquet of mercy.

One thing, and one thing alone, matters to the Beloved,
>that we know each other as the countenance of Christ,
>and bow in deep gratitude for the chance to love. Amen.

Proper 12
Hosea 1:2-10
Psalm 85
Colossians 2:6-15,(16-19)
Luke 11:1-13

Beloved,
may the Wisdom of your abiding Presence
so settle and transform our anxious hearts,
that fear dissolves into courage
and we become a persistent people,
hungry to know You as the heart of all life.
Guide us through the cold shadows
cast by the principalities and powers of this world,
and "do not let surface things delude" our hearts,
focused upon You alone
as the ruling will of life. Amen.

Proper 13
HOSEA 11:1-11
PSALM 107:1-9
COLOSSIANS 3:1-11
LUKE 12:13-21

Beloved Father,
reach out to us,
hold us and lay your kiss upon our trembling hearts.
In our ignorance
    we forget that only as your love incarnate
    are we whole and wholly yours.
In our greed we thrash about,
    hungry for this and for that,
    forgetting that your countenance alone
    stills our hearts.
Stop at nothing, we plead,
to make us your lovers in Christ,
heart and mind and body. Amen.

Feast of Transfiguration
EXODUS 34:29-35
PSALM 99
2 PETER 1:13-21
LUKE 9:28-36

Beloved Mother,
    You give birth to your own image,
    and as You gaze into our eyes
    You marvel that we are so very good.
You, and You alone, are our True Nature.
In Jesus You speak to the depths of our soul,
crying from the Divine Deep –
    "do not settle to be only my image,
    but be transfigured into my holy likeness,
    and be unto me as Christ,
    my only begotten." Amen.

Proper 14
Isaiah 1:1,10-20
Psalm 50:1-8,23-24
Hebrews 11:1-3,8-16
Luke 12:32-40

Beloved Sovereign,
may faith in You rule our heart.
When fear would have us believe
    we are nothing but dust,
        may our heart trust we are Your Love incarnate.
When fear would have us believe
    your call is small and select,
        may our heart trust we are Your Word incarnate.
When fear would have us believe
    You dwell only in a chosen few,
        may our heart trust we are Your Wisdom incarnate.
May Christ *be* our heart,
the Sovereign who rules,
forever and ever. Amen.

Proper 15
Isaiah 5:1-7
Psalm 80:1-2,8-18
Hebrews 11:29-12:2
Luke 12:49-56

Beloved Friend,
You are a Holy Fire
burning away all separateness and division.
May we know You
as the Blaze igniting our souls,
illuminating our union with the great cloud of witnesses,
with whom we work for peace
and stand for justice,
returning all to You,
in whom all are One. Amen.

Proper 16
JEREMIAH 1:4-10
PSALM 71:1-6
HEBREWS 12:18-29
LUKE 13:10-17

Beloved Source,
from your divine womb
all are firstborn, begotten in Love.
When we are bent double
from life's hard, dense, and relentless pain,
hold out your hand to your firstborn
so that we might stretch and stand up straight again.
In You this day
we place the bruised and battered world,
for your unshakeable Will
is that all creatures
be released
from the grip of suffering. Amen.

Proper 17
JEREMIAH 2:4-13
PSALM 81:1,10-16
HEBREWS 13:1-8,15-16
LUKE 14:1,7-14

Beloved One,
the Most Merciful,
in Christ our hearts lie open before You
because forgiving Love, not judgment,
is your True Nature without end.
May the cistern of our hearts
run deep into Deep.
So that when we thirst,
and when angels cross our path in need,
we draw from our heart's Deep,
sharing generously the water of Mercy. Amen.

PROPER 18

JEREMIAH 18:1-11
PSALM 139:1-5,13-18
PHILEMON 1-21
LUKE 14:25-33

Beloved God,
may your Love
so fill our hearts –
    that our thirst is only for You.
May your Faith
so guide our minds –
    that our thoughts are only of You.
May your Wisdom
so saturate our bodies –
    that we live only as You,
    Christ for the world. Amen.

PROPER 19

JEREMIAH 4:11-12,22-28
PSALM 14
1 TIMOTHY 1:12-17
LUKE 15:1-10

Gracious God of eternal embrace,
be Thou our vision:
a faithful community where all are welcome –
    sinner and saint;
be Thou our vision:
a forgiving community where all are renewed –
    foe becomes friend;
be Thou our vision:
a joyous community where all are known and received
    as the beloved of God. Amen.

Proper 20
JEREMIAH 8:18-9:1
PSALM 79:1-9
1 TIMOTHY 2:1-7
LUKE 16:1-13

Beloved,
teach us well
the abiding Truth,
that our ending is the same as our beginning –
gracious union with You.
Joy is lost and our hearts cry in distress,
as we mistake the treasures of this world for You.
Forgive us, Most Merciful One,
and patiently direct our hearts home,
until all our saved and reach full knowledge of the Truth:
the soul's center is God. Amen.

Proper 21
JEREMIAH 32:1-3A,6-15
PSALM 91:1-6,14-16
1 TIMOTHY 6:6-19
LUKE 16:19-31

Most Merciful Redeemer,
unfailing Refuge of all who suffer:
    we often feel overwhelmed,
    unable to receive life's ebb and flow.
    We retreat and build walls,
    seeking to survive by our own sheer strength.
Be unto us the Wisdom
revealing all chasms of separation
as illusions born of fear.
Lower the false gates of our hearts,
and draw us forth into an embrace of creation,
where Christ is all in all. Amen.

Proper 22
Lamentations 1:1-6
Psalm 137
2 Timothy 1:1-14
Luke 17:5-10

Most Merciful One,
how desolate lies our confused heart,
the city of Zion,
when we foolishly seek
to sever our soul from You.
Answer our longing cry
and wipe away the tears of sorrow.
Be unto us the Lord of life –
    your Presence our steadfast strength.
Be the Faith that anchors our life in You,
    now and always. Amen.

Proper 23
Jeremiah 29:1,4-7
Psalm 66:1-11
2 Timothy 2:8-15
Luke 17:11-19

Have pity on us, O Beloved,
    when we feel lost and bewildered,
    and often we do.
Our hearts hunger for home.
    In truth, we hunger for You:
        in whom none is denied;
        in whom none is a foreigner;
        but all are kissed sweetly as friends.
Have pity on us, O Christ.
    Restore us and build our lives anew:
        healed and whole;
        a sanctuary of thanksgiving;
        now and always. Amen.

Proper 24
JEREMIAH 31:27-34
PSALM 119:97-104
2 TIMOTHY 3:14-4:5
LUKE 18:1-8

Beloved Father,
teach us to put on the mind of Christ,
so that we might know all creation,
from beginning to end,
as but a single icon of You.
Beloved Mother,
engrave the love of Christ
as the tender flesh of our heart,
so that we might embrace all creation
from beginning to end,
as your very Body. Amen.

inspired by words of Orthodox theologian, Philip Sherrard,
"All nature, from beginning to end, constitutes a single icon of God."

All Saints
DANIEL 7:1-3,15-18
PSALM 149
EPHESIANS 1:11-23
LUKE 6:20-31

Holy God,
You are nothing
but Truth, Love and Perfection.
May Divine poverty so transform our lives
that like Jesus and the saints,
      we grasp at nothing,
      we cling to nothing,
      we become nothing –
but empty hearts and open minds
ready to receive the fullness of Christ. Amen.

Proper 25

Joel 2:23-32
Psalm 65
2 Timothy 4:6-8,16-18
Luke 18:9-14

Beloved,
the Most Merciful,
let your Spirit rain down upon our flesh,
and wither the proud conceit of our heart.
Then lay our life bare upon the land of your Love,
that we may be fed on knowledge of You,
and realize in all humility,
that when we have died
all that remains is Christ,
whose body we are
and whose Spirit
we breathe. Amen.

Proper 26

Habakkuk 1:1-4,2:1-4
Psalm 119:137-144
2 Thessalonians 1:1-4,11-12
Luke 19:1-10

Holy Wisdom,
there are times when we struggle to see your Presence,
but the outrage of greed and violence
floods our vision and consumes our heart.
> We discover that we grow weary
> from the grip of resentment.

Mother Christ,
teach us to climb above our pettiness
and see your Mercy arising to save what we thought lost.
Receive us back into the world
with hearts grounded anew in You,
> our eyes open,
> > resting upon your healing Presence. Amen.

Proper 27

HAGGAI 1:15B-2:9
PSALM 145:1-5,17-21
2 THESSALONIANS 2:1-5,13-17
LUKE 20:27-38

God of Faith:
may we awaken
to the truth
of your eternal presence with us –
    for in You nothing is lost;
even as the heavens shake loose
all we would hold as certain,
You stand firm –
    the courageous holy Ground of our hearts;
to You we give praise,
not as the God of the dead,
but of the living. Amen.

Proper 28

ISAIAH 65:17-25
CANTICLE 9
2 THESSALONIANS 3:6-13
LUKE 21:5-19

Creating God,
in You is salvation:
    wolf and lamb feed side by side;
    enemies are friends;
    earth is eternally infused with heaven.
Be our patience,
as You continually recreate us,
beloved Jerusalem,
your holy and peaceful habitation. Amen.

Last Sunday after Pentecost – Christ the King

JEREMIAH 23:1-6
CANTICLE 4 OR 16
COLOSSIANS 1:11-20
LUKE 23:33-43

Beloved Sovereign of the universe,
in Jesus is revealed the Royal Way of Christ –
 a heart empty of all fear, deceit, and hatred.
The Way of Christ proclaims your name,
 "Yahweh, Our Justice."
May the Justice of Christ the King
so infuse our hearts, minds, and bodies
that each person we encounter
is beheld as the Royal Divine Presence. Amen.

LITANIES, PRAYERS, BLESSINGS

LITANIES

LITANY OF HEALING

Leader: For souls hardened to rock by arrogance,
All: *River of love, wash over us with simplicity.*

For souls hardened to rock by laziness,
River of love, wash over us with diligence.

For souls hardened to rock by anger,
River of love, wash over us with serenity.

For hearts hardened to rock by pride,
River of love, wash over us with humility.

For hearts hardened to rock by deceit,
River of love, wash over us with truthfulness.

For hearts hardened to rock by envy,
River of love, wash over us with equanimity.

For minds hardened to rock by stinginess,
River of love, wash over us with detachment.

For minds hardened to rock by fear,
River of love, wash over us with courage.

For minds hardened to rock by over-indulgence,
River of love, wash over us with sobriety.

For lives lived behind rock walls of anger, envy, and fear.
River of love, wash over us
 and carry us into You, our life.

PRAYERS

MAY WE

> May we see you, O God,
> > as our own deepest life.
> May we love you, O Christ,
> > as our own beating heart.
> May we know you, O Spirit,
> > as our own true mind.

A NEW HEART

May we forever know you, Adonai,
> as the Most High and Sovereign God,
> because you prove your holiness through all your creatures.

> Take us away from all that is foreign and
> > bring us back home to our own place.

> Sprinkle clean water on us and
> > cleanse us from all our impurities;
> > cleanse us from all our idols.

> Give us a new heart and
> > place within us a new spirit;
> > remove our hearts of stone and
> > give us hearts of flesh.

> Put your Spirit within us and
> > make us live by your statutes,
> > > careful to observe your decrees.

> Empower us to
> > live on this earth, which you gave to our ancestors;
> > > we will be your people,
> > > and you will be our God. Amen.

Based on Ezekiel 36:23-28

BEHOLDING A MESSIAH

Lost and confused, Beloved One,
   we sometimes call out for miracles,
   we sometimes rack our minds.
   Yet, here we stand –
   All: **beholding a messiah nailed to a cross.**

Angry and defensive, Beloved One,
   the cross is at times an obstacle we cannot surmount,
   the cross is at times sheer madness.
   Yet, here we stand –
   All: **beholding a messiah nailed to a cross.**

Silent and listening, Beloved One,
   we receive Christ crucified as *your* wisdom;
   we behold *your* foolishness as wiser than our thoughts;
   we know *your* weakness as stronger than our strength.
   Yet, here we stand –
   All: **beholding a messiah nailed to a cross.**

                                    Based on 1 Cor. 1:.22-25

WHO IS A GOD LIKE YOU?

Who is a God like you,
   pardoning iniquity
   and passing over the transgression of your daughters and sons?
   Who is a God like You?
   All: **Who is a God like You?**

You do not retain your anger forever,
   because you delight in showing clemency.
   Who is a God like You?
   All: **Who is a God like You?**

You will again have compassion upon us;
   you will tread our iniquities under foot.
   Who is a God like You?
   All: **Who is a God like You?**

You will cast all our sins
   into the depths of the sea.
   Who is a God like You?
   All: **Who is a God like You?**
You will show faithfulness to Jacob and Leah
   and unswerving loyalty to Abraham and Sarah,

>   as you have sworn to our ancestors
>   from the days of old.
> Who is a God like You?
> *All:* **Who is a God like You?**
>
> Remind us again this day, O God,
> that what you require of us is but
>   to do justice,
>   and to love kindness,
>   and to walk humbly with you,
>   our God.
> Who is a God like You?
> *All:* **Who is a God like You?**
>
> Based on Micah 7:18-20 and 6:8, NRSV

FREEDOM PRAYER

>   Creating Spirit, we know freedom in You,
>   We surrender ourselves to Your Will.
>
>   Loving Spirit, we know freedom in You,
>   We surrender ourselves to Your Truth.
>
>   Liberating Spirit, we know freedom in You,
>   We surrender ourselves to Your Transformation.
>
> *inspired by the Buddhist Threefold Refuge*

SERENE LIGHT

(sung three times in unison).
>   Serene Light shining as the soul of my being,
>   draw me to yourself.
>   Guide me through the night of the senses,
>   into the darkness beyond the mind.
>   Free from thoughts, plans, memories
>   receiving now each breath.
>   Essence of life unfolding,
>   arising of true Presence.

~Or

Serene Light shining as the soul of my being,
>   *Assembly:* **Serene Light shining as the soul of my being,**

draw me to yourself.
>   *Assembly:* **draw me to yourself.**

draw me to yourself.
>   *Assembly:* **draw me to yourself.**

Guide me through the night of the senses,
>   *Assembly:* **Guide me through the night of the senses,**

into the darkness beyond the mind.
>   *Assembly:* **into the darkness beyond the mind.**

into the darkness beyond the mind.
>   *Assembly:* **into the darkness beyond the mind.**

Free from thoughts, plans, memories
receiving now each breath.
>   *Assembly:* **receiving now each breath.**

Essence of life unfolding,
>   *Assembly:* **Essence of life unfolding,**

Essence of life unfolding,
>   *Assembly*: **Essence of life unfolding,**

arising of true Presence.
>   *Assembly:* **arising of true Presence.**

MAY WE REJOICE

May we rejoice, as sisters and brothers,
>   that our church is persecuted
>   precisely for its preferential option for the poor
>   and for seeking to become incarnate in the interests of the poor.

May we, Your people,
>   stop the repression and stop the killing.

May we, Your people,
>   sacrifice our lives as the seeds of liberty,
>   that who we are and how we live
>   be a sign of hope embodying Christ's resurrection. **Amen.**

inspired by Oscar Romero

WELCOME JESUS

Welcome Jesus, our humble, gentle, Savior,
welcome to Bethlehem
where we have loved and fought
and longed for the peace the world can never give.
We ask for your peace, your love, your gentleness,
and the courage to live that way.

Child of God, child of Mary and Joseph,
born in the stable at Bethlehem,
may we know you as born in us this day.
That through us the world may know
the wonder of your boundless love. **Amen.**

TONIGHT YOU REVEAL

Holy God,
God of Abraham and Sarah and Hagar,
God of Mary and Joseph,
God of Angels and Shepherds,
God of our Beloved, Jesus of Nazareth:
You are God of all the earth.
Tonight you reveal to us again
that all people are your beloved children
and that all creatures are your handiwork.
Let us never cease to tell the story
of your boundless love
in all we say and do. **Amen.**

GOD OF HOPE AND PROMISE

: God of hope and promise:
Through your love
    the promise of life enfolds our hearts;
In your heart
    we offer our lives in hope;
And so,
As the morning Star eternally sings your praises -
    we lay in your open hands
    the thankful prayers of our selves, our souls,
our bodies. **Amen.**

HOLOCAUST PRAYER: CREATE IN US CLEAN HEARTS, O GOD

Leader: God of Abraham, Sarah and Hagar,
Assembly: **God of Isaiah, Ruth and Ezekiel,**
Leader: God of Jesus, Mohammad and Bahá'u'lláh
Assembly: **God, Creator and Wisdom of the universe:**

Leader: Awaken us to know that each and every person
is created in your image and called to become your very likeness.
Assembly: **Create in us clean hearts, O God.**

Leader: Transfigure the deceit,
whereby tribes and religions would mold you in their image.
May we know and live the sacred truth of your
Presence in all peoples and faiths.
Assembly: **Create in us clean hearts, O God.**

Leader: Transfigure the fear,
whereby we are paralyzed into bystanders
watching the destruction of your holy ones.
May we become, like Holy Wisdom,
people of unfailing courage, regardless of the cost.
Assembly: **Create in us clean hearts, O God.**

Leader: Transfigure the numbness,
whereby we remain content in our ignorance
of suffering, of holocaust.
May we become a powerful people
of self-less love;
May we be united in our awareness
that we live, move, breathe
and have our being
only in You. **Amen.**

ASH WEDNESDAY:
A WAY THROUGH THE WILDERNESS

Presider Let us pray together:
**Jesus,
You are the way through the wilderness:
show us your truth in which we journey,
and by the grace of the Holy Spirit
be in us the life that draws us to God. Amen.**

Prayers of the People

Form: Loving Spirit

Like a warrior you fight tirelessly for peace in the world; may we know you as the strength of our hearts, granting us the courage to live together in justice and faith. Loving Spirit,
God most merciful, we are yours.

Like an elder you offer vision and wisdom to illumine the path of the members of our episcopal ministry support team; may they know you as the Guide, grounding them in prayer, and giving them courage, wisdom, listening hearts, creativity, and a willingness to risk; may they know they have been chosen to serve. Loving Spirit,
God most merciful, we are yours.

Like a mother you enfold all children and young people; may they know you as their guide through life's challenges and opportunities. Loving Spirit,
God most merciful, we are yours.

Like a father you protect all those who are sick [especially_____]; may they know you as their deliverer, carrying them when their own hearts fail. Loving Spirit,
God most merciful, we are yours.

Like a friend and lover you bring hope to all those who are condemned to exile, prison, harsh treatment, or hard labor, for the sake of justice and truth; may they find comfort in your promise and rest in your presence. Loving Spirit,
God most merciful, we are yours.

Like a breath of freedom, you choose prophets, apostles, martyrs, and all who have borne witness to the gospel of uncompromising love [especially_____]; may we know you as the Truth directing our own lives in the same spirit of service, sacrifice and celebration. Loving Spirit,
God most merciful, we are yours.

Presider: Creator of the universe,
by your Loving Spirit you make us one
with your saints in heaven and on earth.
In our earthly pilgrimage
may we know ourselves

	supported by this company of love and prayer,

                  supported by this company of love and prayer,
                  and surrounded by the great cloud of witnesses.
                  We ask this
                  trusting in your endless mercy
                  revealed to us in Jesus Christ,
                  Spirit made flesh.

All: **Amen.**

Form: We Are Grateful

In gratitude, we offer our grateful hearts, minds, and bodies, to You, God of Life.
Silence

In gratitude for all people in their daily life and work;
We are grateful for our families, friends, and neighbors, and for all your creatures.

In gratitude for this community, the nation, and the world;
We are grateful for all who work for justice, freedom, and peace.

In gratitude for the witness of those who suffer from hunger, fear, injustice, and oppression;
We are grateful for all who hear the call to honor, nurture, and share, the gifts of creation and community.

In gratitude for the perseverance of those in danger, sorrow, or any kind of trouble;
We are grateful for those who walk with us in our sickness, loneliness, and need.

In gratitude for the peace and unity of the church;
We are grateful for all who listen to your Word, proclaim the Gospel, and seek the Truth.

In gratitude for *N* our Presiding Bishop, for *N* our Bishop, for the Episcopal Ministry Support Team, and for all who minister;
We are grateful for all whose hearts burn with the Spirit's desire to serve.

In gratitude for the special needs and concerns of this congregation.
Our hearts speak their gratefulness.

In gratitude for the blessing of your love.
Our hearts speak their gratefulness.

In gratitude we exalt You, our Beloved, the God of Life;
And gratefully praise your Name for ever and ever.

In gratitude we remember all who have died, grateful for their place in your eternal kingdom.
Our hearts remember the beloved ones of our lives.

Presider:	In gratitude for your loving-kindness
	that rains down upon all creatures.
	In gratitude for your acceptance
	of the grateful prayers of your people.
	In gratitude for your compassion
	upon us and all who turn to You for help.
	You are gracious, O God of Life,
	and to You we give glory,
	now and for ever.
All:	**Amen.**

Inspired by "Form VI" of The Book of Common Prayer

FORM: LITANY FOR BAPTISMAL MINISTRY

Three pitchers of water are brought forward. As a pitcher of water is poured into the baptismal font, the litany begins.

Like an elder, You offer vision and wisdom to illumine the path of the Church, of our Diocese, of N, our bishop, and of all the baptized; may we know You as the guide, grounding us in prayer, and giving us courage, wisdom, listening hearts, creativity, and a willingness to risk; may we know we have been chosen to serve, Loving Spirit;
Pour your Life into our hearts.

May we encourage and support one another in our many and
various ministries, seeking always to be faithful stewards of the
gifts You bestow all creatures, Loving Spirit;
Pour your Life into our hearts.

May we hold in trust the questioning mind, the searching heart,
the thirsting soul, guarding as sacred the many different paths
into you, the Font of all Life, Loving Spirit;
Pour your Life into our hearts.

May we be as ready to hear the good news from your people of
other denominations and faiths, as we are to proclaim the
Gospel, healing our false divisions, celebrating our diversity, and
pursuing our common mission, Loving Spirit;
Pour your Life into our hearts.

Water is poured from the second pitcher into the baptismal font.

Like a mother, You enfold all children and young people; may they know
You as their unfailing peace amidst life's challenges and opportunities,
Loving Spirit;
Wash away the prison of fear.

May we worship you in body, mind, and heart, celebrating
together the joy of your presence in all creation, Loving Spirit;
Wash away the prison of fear.

May we lay all that we are and all that we have in your hands,
trusting in your redeeming love to mend our brokenness,
Loving Spirit;
Wash away the prison of fear.

May we forever know You as our heart's deepest desire, opening your
gracious table to all who hunger and thirst, Loving Spirit;
Wash away the prison of fear.

Water is poured from the third pitcher into the baptismal font.

Like a warrior, You fight tirelessly for peace in our nation and the world;
may we know You as the strength of our hearts, granting us the courage
to honor and celebrate the beauty and dignity of every human being,
Loving Spirit;
Unleash the waters of your justice.

May we come to see Christ in all your creatures, being ready to honor, help and serve those in need, Loving Spirit;
Unleash the waters of your justice.

May we know ourselves to be created in your triune image of Creator, Redeemer and Sanctifier, restoring wholeness in your creation – beautiful, yet broken through ignorance, greed and fear, Loving Spirit;
Unleash the waters of your justice.

May we hear, receive, and know your Word, becoming a people set free in love to lift the yoke of racism from the neck of your children, Loving Spirit;
Unleash the waters of your justice.

Like a father, You protect all those who are sick [especially_____]; may they know You as their deliverer, carrying them when their own hearts fail, Loving Spirit;
Wash us, renew us, we are yours.

Like a friend and lover, You bring hope to all those who are condemned to exile, prison, harsh treatment, or hard labor, for the sake of justice and truth; may they find comfort in your promise and rest in your presence, Loving Spirit;
Wash us, renew us, we are yours.

Like a breath of freedom, You choose prophets, apostles, martyrs, and all who have borne witness to the gospel of uncompromising love [especially those we remember now_____]; may we know You as the Truth directing our own lives in the same spirit of service, sacrifice and celebration, Loving Spirit;
Wash us, renew us, we are yours.

BLESSINGS

FOREVER LOVING, BEAUTIFUL, AND GOOD

Presider: May the blessing of God,
forever Loving, Beautiful, and Good,
draw you forth into lives of justice and peace,
this day and always.
Assembly: **Amen.**

CHRIST, OUR OWN HEART

Presider: As we go forth from this place
into God's creation,
may we be blessed with the knowledge that
Christ is before us,
    to lead the way;
Christ is above us,
    as our shade;
Christ is behind us,
    to protect us;
Christ is beneath us,
    as our strength;
Christ is within us,
our own Heart,
this day and always.
Assembly: **Amen.**

THE GREAT THREE DAYS

DAY ONE
MAUNDY THURSDAY: SENT TO SERVE

Presider Let us pray together:
   Beloved,
   life is a banquet
   overflowing from the heart of your dance of Love.
   On this night,
   The Lover has annihilated Jesus.
   Now Love alone remains,
   who invites all to the table
   spread upon the sea of generosity.
   Freely, Love pours forth life.
   This Soul is free, supremely free,
   in the stock,
   in all her branches
   and all the fruits of her braches.
   Nothing but sweet flowing wine remains
   and the Soul says:
   Drink this, all of you:
   This is my life Blood
   a joyous Covenant from which flows
   forgiveness of sin and life renewed.
   Remember, you can be no less for me. Amen.

Washing & Anointing of Hands for Service

Presider:
   Jesus supped with his disciples
   and washed their feet.
   Afterwards, he said to them:
   Do you know what I,
   your Lord and Master,
   have done to you?
   I have given you an example,
   that you should do as I have done.

Assembly:
> **Peace is my last gift to you,**
> **my own peace I now leave with you;**
> **peace which the world cannot give, I give to you.**

Presider:
> I give you a new commandment:
> Love one another as I have loved you.

Assembly:
> **Peace is my last gift to you,**
> **my own peace I now leave with you;**
> **peace which the world cannot give, I give to you.**

Presider:
> By this shall the world know that you are my disciples:
> That you have love for one another.
>
> I invite you forward.
>
> *Please come forward to the baptismal waters for washing and anointing of hands for service. The presbyter will wash with the words: "You are washed by Christ in the waters of baptism." The deacon will anoint with the words: "These are the hands of Christ, anointed for service."*

Day Two
Good Friday – The cycle of Suffering Ceases: Almighty and All-Compassionate God

Presider:	Blessed be our God,
Assembly:	**For ever and ever. Amen.**
Presider:	Beloved Creator,
	we, your very own,
	created in your image
	and called to become your likeness,
	become blinded
	by our ignorance, fear, anger and greed.
	This sinful veil blinds us
	to your beauty embodied in neighbor and creation.
	We stand before you
	with your mercy raining down upon us,
	washing over our lives with renewing forgiveness.
	Be the grace
	that strengthens us to serve you in newness of life,
	to the glory of your name.
Presider:	Let us pray together:
	Gracious God,
	turn the gaze of our souls to
	Jesus, the Beloved,
	heart of our heart,
	whose beauty was broken open upon the cross:
	may Christ's arms embrace our broken lives;
	may Christ's heart heal our tortured world;
	and may the sinful veil
	of ignorance, fear, anger and greed
	be lifted from our eyes,
	so that we might see
	and fall into the Beloved's boundless mercy. Amen.

Solemn Collects

We stand as able.

Presider:
>Dear People of God:
>Jesus of Nazareth,
>God's Beloved,
>embodies the Wisdom way of life.
>Jesus reveals the path of salvation
>to all who would see and receive.
>Jesus is the light of life
>in the midst of suffering, darkness and death.
>Born of the one God in Christ,
>we too are heirs of everlasting life.
>We pray with gratitude, therefore, for people everywhere.

Presider:
>Let us pray in thanksgiving for the holy Catholic Church of Christ throughout the world;
>>For its unity in witness and service
>>For all who minister and the people and creation whom they serve
>>For our *N,* our bishop, and (other ministerial leaders)
>>For all the people of this diocese
>>For all members in this community
>>For those about to be baptized.
>
>With grateful hearts that God confirms the Church in faith, increases it in love, and preserves it in peace.

Silence

All:
>**Beloved God,**
>**your Spirit,**
>**source of life and hope,**
>**weaves us together as one body,**
>**dwelling in You.**
>**Our selves, our souls, our bodies,**
>**are your very Presence.**
>**We offer all to You in thanksgiving.**
>**Be unto us this day the path of life,**
>**so that all that we are**
>**and all that we do,**
>**serves you, our neighbor, and all creation,**
>**through Christ our Lord. Amen.**

Presider:
>Let us pray in thanksgiving for all nations and peoples of the earth, and for those in authority;
>>For N, the President of the United States
>>For the Congress and the Supreme Court
>>For the Members and Representatives of the United Nations
>>For all who serve the common good.
>
>With grateful hearts that by God's help they can seek justice and truth, and live in peace and concord.

Silence

All:
>**Beloved God,**
>**we offer praise and thanksgiving,**
>**for the flame of your Holy Presence**
>**that ignites hearts to burn for justice and peace;**
>**for the light of your Holy Wisdom**
>**that guides minds in compassionate counsel for the nations of the earth;**
>**may fire of Holy Love so consume the dross of our lives**
>**that nothing remains on earth or in heaven**
>**but the love of Christ,**
>**all in all. Amen.**

Presider:
>Let us pray in thanksgiving for all who suffer and are afflicted in body or in mind;
>>For the hungry and the homeless, the destitute and the oppressed
>>For the sick, the wounded, and the crippled
>>For those in loneliness, fear, and anguish
>>For those who are driven by doubt or despair
>>For the sorrowful and bereaved
>>For prisoners and captives, and those in mortal danger
>
>With grateful hearts that God's mercy is comfort and relief, and that knowledge of divine love stirs up in us the will and patience to minister to the needs of our sisters and brothers.

Silence

All:
>Beloved God,
>Source of all Creation,
>comfort of all who sorrow,
>
>strength of all who suffer:
>May those in misery and need come to you
>and find your mercy present within them
>in all their afflictions.
>Be unto us the constancy that steadies our souls
>to persevere in service to all in need,
>for all indeed are Christ. Amen.

Presider:
>Let us pray in thanksgiving for all who search for God;
>For all of us who have fallen asleep to life
>For all of us consumed by anger
>For all of us swollen by pride
>For all of us misled by deceit
>For all of us obsessed by envy
>For all of us driven by greed
>For all of us trapped by fear
>For all of us deceived by gluttony
>For all of us hounded by revenge
>With grateful hearts that God opens all hearts to unfolding truth.

Silence

All:
>Beloved God,
>Let us commit ourselves to the Wisdom way.
>Let us open our hearts to receive the grace of a holy life.
>Let us come to know the fullness and joy of Christ.
>In birth we are born in Christ.
>In death we die in Christ.
>In resurrection we live in Christ.
>
>All is given by You
>as a taste of the Beloved Christ.
>May we joyously receive. Amen.

Silence

Presider:
>Beloved God,
>"Everything looks to You, without thinking.
>Shower us with Your Healing Rain!
>Help us to overcome, give life to what has withered.
>And water the roots of kindness in us." *

All: **Amen.**

Meditation – The Wisdom Way of the Cross

Presider:
>Jesus –
>>open arms,
>>>open table,
>>>>God's love embracing all.
>
>Jesus –
>>love of God,
>>>love of neighbor,
>>>>no compromise, no condition,
>>>>>Rome's cross.

Assembly:
>**Come. Let us be the body of Christ**
>**and follow love's Wisdom way.**

We may come forward in silence and light a candle beside the cross.

* *inspired by Jinjing,* <u>The Jesus Sutras</u>, *and Meister Eckhart*

Day Three
The Easter Vigil: Celebration of Life Renewed

The Fire of Life

We stand as able.

Presider: Blessed are you, Lord God of all creation,
to you be glory and praise for ever.
Your steadfast love extends to the heavens
and your faithfulness never ceases.
Illuminate our hearts with your wisdom
and strengthen our lives with your word,
for you are the fountain of life;
in your light we see true light.
We make our prayer in Jesus Christ.

All: **Amen.**

Deacon: This is the night in which our Lord Jesus Christ passes over from death to life. We gather to listen to the record of God's saving work in history and today, recalling how She saves her people and is Manifest in Jesus, our Redeemer. And we pray that through this Easter celebration God may bring to perfection in each of us the saving work She has begun. This is the Passover of the Lord! We share in Christ's victory over death.

Presider: Jesus Christ, you are the light of the world;
Choir: **the light no darkness can overcome;**
Presider: Stay with us now for it is evening,
Choir: **and the day is almost over.**
Presider: Let your light scatter the darkness
Choir: **and shine within your people here.**

The New Fire is Kindled in the Darkness

Welcoming and Sending Forth Members

WELCOMING NEW MEMBERS

Presider: Each of us is created in the image of God
and gathered by a love
that knows no bounds.

N: Love is my chosen food, my cup,
holding me in its power.
Where I have come from,
where're I shall go,
love is my birthright
my true estate.
                                            (Psalm 16)

Presider: As a community of faith,
we seek and serve Christ in all creation.
As a community of hope,
we respect the dignity of all God's creatures.
As a community of love,
we hold *your* life and journey as sacred.

N: I bless the Counselor
who guides my way.
                                            (Psalm 16)

All: **N,**
we welcome you into
<u>**St. Paul's**</u> **community of faith.**
We embrace your gifts –
may they enliven us
      to "walk beside the Spirit of Truth";
may they invite us
      to "celebrate the Light";
may they challenge us
      to grow in Christ
in unimaginable ways. Amen.

SENDING FORTH A MEMBER

Presider: Beloved Companion,
wondrously show your steadfast love.
O Love Divine,
walk beside me as my strength;
keep me the apple of your eye.   (Psalm 17)

N: Open my heart that compassion may be my companion;
Where I meet pride, humble me.
Where I meet anger, calm my fears.
Where I meet injustice, cause me to act in love's way.
    (Psalm 17)

Presider: As a community of faith,
we seek and serve Christ in all creation.
As a community of hope,
we respect the dignity of all God's creatures.
As a community of love,
we hold *your* life and journey as sacred.

N: I bless the Counselor
who guides my way.   (Psalm 16)

All: **N,**
We have been deeply blessed
    by your gifts,
    by your care,
    by your friendship.
We send you forth from
<u>*St. Paul's*</u> **community of faith.**
We hope that those who receive you
embrace your gifts –
    may you enliven them
        to "walk beside the Spirit of Truth";
    may you invite them
        to "celebrate the Light";
    may you receive them as your
        friends in Christ;
        and grow together
        in unimaginable ways. Amen.

Baptismal Covenant

Gathering

Presider: Blessed be God,
beloved Creator, Redeemer and Sanctifier.
Assembly: **And blessed be God's glorious reign,
now and for ever. Amen.**

Presider: There is one Body and one Spirit;
Assembly: **There is one hope in God's call to us;**
Presider: One Lord, one Faith, one Baptism;
Assembly: **One God and Father of all.**
Presider: The Lord is with you.
Assembly: **And also with you.**
Presider: Let us pray together
**In water are we conceived.
In water are we knit together in the Spirit.
Through the breaking of water are we born.
Through the drinking of water are we nourished.
You, O God,** *are* **the living water:
wash over us, again and again and again,
that in Christ we might live
as your daughters and sons,
and that with Christ as our heart
we might respect the dignity of every human being.
Amen.**

The service continues as usual until the time appointed for baptism.

The Presentation for Baptism

Presider: The Candidate for Holy Baptism
will now be presented.

Parents and Godparents:
I present N to receive the Sacrament of Baptism

Presider: Will you be responsible for seeing that N
is brought up in the Christian faith and life?

Parents and Godparents:
I will, with God's help.

Presider: Will you, by your prayers and witness, help
N to grow into the full stature of Christ?

Parents and Godparents:
I will, with God's help.

Presider: Do you seek to awaken to the eternal
presence of God,
who is your very heart and soul?

Parents and Godparents:
I do.

Presider: God forever invites you
to let go of self deceit
to dwell in the house of honesty,
where eternal Hope reigns.
Will you accept this invitation?

Parents and Godparents:
I will, with God's help.

Presider: God forever invites you
to let go of all fear
to dwell in the house of courage,
where eternal Faith reigns.
Will you accept this invitation?

Parents and Godparents:
I will, with God's help.

Presider: God forever invites you
to let go of all anger
to dwell in the house of serenity,
where Love reigns.

	Will you accept this invitation?
Parents and Godparents:	**I will, with God's help.**
Presider:	Do you turn to Jesus Christ and accept him as the way of Life and Hope?
Parents and Godparents:	**I do.**
Presider:	Do you put your whole trust in Christ's grace and love?
Parents and Godparents:	**I do.**
Presider:	Do you promise to follow Christ as the way of life?
Parents and Godparents:	**I do.**

We stand as able.

Presider:	Will you who witness these vows do all in your power to support N in her life in Christ?
Assembly:	**We will.**
Presider:	Let us join with those who are committing themselves to Christ and renew our own baptismal covenant.

The Renewal of Baptismal Vows

Presider:	Do you place the trust of your heart in God, the Source of life?
Assembly:	**God, Creator of heaven and earth,** **I place the trust of my heart in You.**
Presider:	Do you place the trust of your heart in God, the Word of life?
Assembly:	**God, Love incarnate,** **Jesus Christ our Lord,** **I place the trust of my heart in You.** **You were conceived by the Holy Spirit,**

>   born of the Virgin Mary,
>   suffered under Pontius Pilate,
>   crucified, died, and buried,
>   You descended to the dead.
>   You arose again on the third day.
>   You ascended into heaven.
>   You are seated at the right hand of God,
>   and will come again
>   to judge the living and the dead.

Presider: Do you place the trust of your heart in God, the Breath of life?

Assembly: **God, Holy Spirit,**
I place the trust of my heart in You,
in the holy catholic Church,
in the communion of saints,
in the forgiveness of sins,
in the resurrection of the body,
and the life everlasting.

Presider: Will you continue in the apostles' teaching and fellowship, in the breaking of the bread, and in the prayers?

Assembly: **I will, with God's help.**

Presider: Will you persevere in resisting evil, and, whenever you fall into sin, repent and return to God?

Assembly: **I will, with God's help.**

Presider: Will you proclaim by word and example the Good News of God in Christ?

Assembly: **I will, with God's help.**

Presider: Will you seek and serve Christ in all persons, loving your neighbor as yourself?

Assembly: **I will, with God's help.**

Presider: Will you strive for justice and peace among all people, and respect the dignity of every human being?

Assembly: **I will, with God's help.**

Presider: May we always know that all creation rests eternally in the compassionate arms of God, the Mother and Father of all, who ceaselessly gives new birth

	by water and the Holy Spirit,

                  by water and the Holy Spirit,
                  who forever bestows upon us
                  the forgiveness of sin,
                  and who graciously keeps all creation
                  forever in eternal life,
                  living in the heart of Christ.

Assembly: **Amen.**

Prayers of the People

Presider: As we celebrate the Sacrament of rebirth,
let us pray for the church, the world and N:

Leader: May all who confess your Name
be united in your truth,
live together in your love,
and reveal your glory in the world. Lord
hear our prayer.

Leader: May the people of this land,
and of all the nations,
be guided in your ways of justice and peace;
that we may honor one another
and serve the common good. Lord,
hear our prayer.

Leader: May all those who suffer in body, mind, or spirit be comforted and healed;
may they find courage and hope in their troubles, and the joy of your salvation. Lord,
hear our prayer.

Leader: May all who have died receive your mercy,
that your will for them may be fulfilled;
and may we share with all your saints
in your eternal kingdom. Lord,
hear our prayer.

Leader: May N know your Spirit
as the faith liberating *her*
from the broken and deadly way
of anger, fear, and deceit. Lord,
hear our prayer.

Leader:	May N know your Spirit as the love opening *her* to your grace and truth. Lord, **hear our prayer.**
Leader:	May N know your Spirit as the hope filling *her* soul with wholeness and life. Lord, **hear our prayer.**
Leader:	May N know that *she* forever has a place in the faith and communion of your holy Church. Lord, **hear our prayer.**
Leader:	May N learn to love others in the power of the Spirit. Lord, **hear our prayer.**
Leader:	May N know that *she* is sent into the world in witness to your love. Lord, **hear our prayer.**
Leader:	May N know that in you is the fullness of peace and glory. Lord, **hear our prayer.**
Presider:	You, O God, grant that all who are baptized into the death of Jesus live in the power of the resurrection, and look for Christ to come again in glory; who lives and reigns in love now and for ever.
All:	**Amen.**

We sit.

Thanksgiving over the Water

Presider:	The Lord is with you.
Assembly:	**And also with you.**
Presider:	Let us give thanks to the Lord our God.
Assembly:	**It is right to give God thanks and praise.**
Presider:	We thank you, Father, for the gift of water.
	Your Holy Spirit moves over water i n the beginning of creation.

You lead the children of Israel out of their bondage in Egypt through water into the land of promise.

Your child Jesus goes down into the waters to receive the baptism of John and is anointed by the Holy Spirit as the Messiah, the Christ, to lead us, through his death and resurrection, from the bondage of sin into everlasting life.

We thank you, Mother, for the water of Baptism.

We are buried in these waters with Christ in his death.

Through these waters we share in Christ's resurrection.

Through these waters we are reborn by the Holy Spirit.

Therefore as joyful followers of the way of Christ, we bring into the company of saints those who come to Christ in faith, baptizing them in the name of the one God who is always and everywhere creating, redeeming and sanctifying us.

You sanctify this water by the power of your Holy Spirit that those who here are received into this household may continue for ever in the risen life of

Jesus Christ our Savior. To Christ, to You, and to the Holy Spirit, be all honor and glory, now and for ever.

All: **Amen.**

The Baptism

Presider: N, I baptize you in the name of the Father,
and of the Son, and of the Holy Spirit.
All: **Amen.**

Presider: N, you are sealed by the Holy Spirit in Baptism
and marked as Christ's own for ever.
All: **Amen.**

Presider: Beloved God,
we thank you that by water and the Holy Spirit
you welcome N into the church,
you bestow upon this your beloved
the forgiveness of sin,

and raise her to the new life of grace.
May she know you, O God,
as the Spirit sustaining her.
May she know you, O God,
as her own inquiring and discerning heart.
May she know you, O God,
as her own courage and love;
and may she taste your joy and wonder, O God,
in all she does.

All: **Amen.**

EUCHARISTIC PRAYERS

EUCHARISTIC PRAYER OF THE ABIDING WORD

Presider: The Lord is with you.
Assembly: **And also with you.**
Presider: Lift up your hearts.
Assembly: **We lift them to the Lord.**
Presider: Let us give thanks to the Lord our God.
Assembly: **It is right to give God thanks and praise.**
Presider: It is truly right, and good and joyful, to give you thanks, all-holy God, source of life and fountain of mercy. You fill us and all creation with your blessing and feed us with your constant love; you redeem us in Jesus Christ and knit us into one body. Through your Spirit you replenish us and call us to fullness of life. Therefore, joining with Angels and Archangels and with the faithful of every generation, we lift our voices with all creation as we sing:

Sanctus

Presider: Blessed are you, gracious God,
Creator of the universe and source of life.
You form us in your own image
and call us to become your very likeness.

In you are we free to care for creation;
in you are we courageous to continue our journey;
in you are our hearts radiant with your grace.

Even though your grace and peace are always in us,
we often fail to live in your grace and peace.
Confused and lost we fail to honor your image
in one another, in ourselves and in all creation;
blind to your goodness saturating the world,
We grow angry, deceitful and afraid.
Yet your abiding Word continues to call out to us
from the very center of creation.

Your Word never ceases to remind us
of your unflagging devotion.
Your Word bids us return to the path
of wholeness and healing.

Through matriarchs, patriarchs, and prophets we hear
your Word call us into covenant with you.
You invite us out of slavery
and offer sustenance in the wilderness.

In Jesus is your Word again
born anew among us as flesh.
Beloved, living within our midst,
Jesus is your eternal love manifest.
Rather than restrict the bounty of your grace,
your Beloved willingly accepts
  Roman death on the cross.
Refusing the lure of vengeful retribution,
your Beloved reveals the
  power of compassion in the face of evil.
In Jesus' death you make known
the divine path of freedom and life.

On the night before he dies,
Jesus takes bread,
gives thanks to you,
breaks it, gives it to his friends and says:
take, eat,
this is my Body I give for you.
Do this for the remembrance of me.

As supper is ending, Jesus takes the cup of wine,
again gives you thanks,
gives it to his friends and says:
drink this, all of you:
this is my Blood of the new Covenant,
which I pour out for you and for all
for the forgiveness of sin.
Whenever you drink it,
do this for the remembrance of me.

Gathered in you, O God,
we remember Jesus' death and resurrection,
and present to you from your creation,

| | this bread and this wine.
| | By your Holy Spirit may we receive them as
| | the Body and Blood of the Beloved.
| | Grant that we who share these gifts
| | may know ourselves
| | to be filled with the Holy Spirit
| | and live as Christ's Body in the world.

Born anew this day as your daughter and sons,
in the company of the saints,
    past, present, and yet to come,
our hearts rejoice in praise of your Name.
Through Christ and with Christ and in Christ,
in the unity of the Holy Spirit,
to you be honor, glory, and praise,
for ever and ever.

All: **AMEN.**

Presider: As our Savior Christ has taught us, we now pray,

All: **Our Father in heaven,**
hallowed be your name.
Your kingdom come.
Your will be done on earth and in heaven.
Give us today the bread of life.
Forgive us our sins
as we forgive those who sin against us.
Save us from the time of trial
and deliver us from evil.
For the kingdom, the power,
and the glory are yours,
now and for ever. Amen.

The Breaking of the Bread

Presider: We break this bread
to share in the Body of Christ.
Assembly: **We who are many are one body,**
for we all share in the one bread.
Presider: The Gifts of God for the People of God.
All are invited to God's table.

inspired by the work of Julian of Norwich and Meister Eckhart
The version of the Lord's Prayer is from St. Gregory of Nyssa, San Francisco, CA

Eucharistic Prayer of Celebration of Creation

Presider: The Lord is with you.
Assembly: **And also with you.**
Presider: Lift up your hearts.
Assembly: **We lift them to the Lord.**
Presider: You are Life, sustaining and beckoning us home.
Assembly: **We sing your praise to the highest heavens.**

Presider: Beloved Creator,
in You the Universe is born,
and manifests your glory from age to age.
You are Life, sustaining and beckoning us home.
Assembly: **We sing your praise to the highest heavens.**

Presider: From You pours forth
the surprising unfolding of life:
from creatures of the sea
to the quasars and black holes
of ever expanding space.
You are Life, sustaining and beckoning us home.
Assembly: **We sing your praise to the highest heavens.**

Presider: Your Spirit permeates all creation
and if the rocks could find voice even they would cry
out in endless gratitude; hearts, minds, and bodies, all
reflect your glory.
Yet, as we grow, your Presence, nearer than our own
breath,
fades and fades;
we grow blind and long for your face to press against
ours once more;
the song of our hearts searches for the Beloved.
You are Life, sustaining and beckoning us home.
Assembly: **We sing your praise to the highest heavens.**

Presider: We fall. We rise. We betray. We reconcile.
All we do is done in You.
You are Life, sustaining and beckoning us home.
Assembly: **We sing your praise to the highest heavens.**

Sanctus

Presider: You teach us, dear God,
to wait upon You in every present moment
and receive your renewal in our lives.
You redeem us by water and Spirit,
awakening us to know
that because all things are consonant with You,
our souls find You in all things.

Beloved Creator,
may our hearts reverberate with the truth
that You are more in us
than if the sea
could be wholly contained
in a single sponge.

Saturated with your Presence,
we bring before You
these sacred gifts of your earth.
Sanctify them by your Holy Spirit,
for they are the Body and Blood of Jesus Christ our Lord.
You are Life, sustaining and beckoning us home.

Assembly: **We sing your praise to the highest heavens.**

Presider: On the night Jesus suffered and died,
your Beloved took bread,
gave thanks to You, broke it,
and gave it to the disciples, and said,
take, eat: this is my Body, which is given for you.
Do this for the remembrance of me.

After supper Jesus took the cup of wine,
gave thanks, gave it to them, and said,
drink this, all of you:
this is my Blood of the new Covenant,
which is shed for you and for many for the forgiveness
of sin.
Whenever you drink it,
do this for the remembrance of me.

God of our Ancestors;
God of Abraham, Sarah, and Hagar,

	Isaac and Rebecca, Jacob, Leah and Rachel; God of Jesus Christ: Open our eyes to see your Presence unfolding in the world and may the grace of these sacred earthly fruits, bread and wine, nourish and enfold us forever into one body, one Spirit, in Christ.
	Eternal Font of life, love, and hope, born of your Spirit and renewed in Christ we sing forth your praises, giving You all honor and glory, this day and always. You are Life, sustaining and beckoning us home.
Assembly:	**We sing your praise to the highest heavens.**
Presider:	As our Savior Christ has taught us, we now pray,
All:	**Our Father in heaven, hallowed be your name. Your kingdom come. Your will be done on earth and in heaven. Give us today the bread of life. Forgive us our sins as we forgive those who sin against us. Save us from the time of trial and deliver us from evil. For the kingdom, the power, and the glory are yours, now and for ever. Amen.**

The Breaking of the Bread

Presider:	We break this bread to share in the Body of Christ.
Assembly:	**We who are many are one body, for we all share in the one bread.**
Presider:	The Gifts of God for the People of God. All are invited to God's table.

inspired by the work of
Margarete Porete, Meister Eckhart,
Angelus Silesius, Jürgen Moltmann,
Nicholas Cusa, and Eucharistic Prayer C.
The version of the Lord's Prayer is from St. Gregory of Nyssa, San Francisco, CA

Eucharistic Prayer of Nativity

Presider:	The Lord is with you
Assembly:	**And also with you**
Presider:	Lift up your hearts
Assembly:	**We lift them to the Lord**
Presider:	Let us give thanks to the Lord our God
Assembly:	**It is right to give God thanks and praise.**

All: Holy God, source of life and without end,
   we give thanks to you!
You continually call all life into being,
   cradling your creation in compassion.
You spread out the heavens like a tent
   and enclose the seas.
You fill the world with wondrous creatures
   and know all things as truly good.
You send your heavenly messengers of hope
   day and night,
   and with them we sing and give glory to you:

Sanctus *Santo, Santo, Santo*

Presider: In the days of Simeon and Anna,
   you leaned toward the earth.
Your eternal Spirit became known to us
   through your Beloved.
Born into the family of Mary and Joseph,
Jesus was cradled beside the beasts
   and warmed by their breath –
Here was your child, like all your children,
   woven into life by the Spirit
   and in need of compassion.
Worldly rulers
   were troubled by your dawning reign –
   embodied in this child,
   in whom the fullness of your Spirit
   was pleased to dwell.

Assembly: **All is born of your Spirit, Creating God.**
All is full of your grace, Loving God
All is beautiful – yet broken through fear, anger
and deceit -- Liberating God.

Presider: As your Beloved servant,
Jesus became empty of might upon the cross.
As the Risen Anointed One,
Jesus is forever embraced by you as Christ,
    embodying your eternal mercy and
    restoring justice to all the earth,
    now and forever.

Assembly   **And so,**
        together we stand,
            rejoicing in all that you,
                All-loving God,
                      have done
    and continue to do for us.

Holy God,
as you visited us in the birth of Jesus,
heal our blindness
so that we may see your Presence now
always within and among us.
In these delightful creatures of bread and wine
    – holy food and holy drink –
help us to taste the banquet of heaven here on earth.

Presider: We remember how Jesus took bread,
blessed, broke it and gave it to his friends saying,
take, eat, this is my body given for you,
do this for the remembrance of me.
Likewise, the Beloved held the cup of wine,
blessed it and gave it to them saying,
drink this, all of you.
This cup is the covenant in my blood,
poured out for you and for many,
that you may know God
always holds you in tender forgiveness.
Do this for the remembrance of me.

All: **Holy God,**
you shed your grace
brighter than starlight on us,
that our hearts may radiate
your good tidings to all
and renew the weary world in your name:
Emmanuel, God-With-Us,
to whom we give honor and glory in joy,
now and forever. Amen!!

Eucharistic Prayer of Swimming in the Sea of Joy

Presider: Love is you.
Assembly: **And also you.**
Presider: Love raises our joyous hearts unto God.
Assembly: **For Love is God and God is Love.**
Presider: Our Souls cry out with thanks to God, our Love.
Assembly: **We live in God alone, for nothing else remains in Love's bright burning.**

Presider: As daughters and sons of Zion,
we neither desire
nor despise poverty nor tribulation,
neither mass nor sermon,
neither fast nor prayer.
We give to Nature all that is necessary,
without remorse of conscience.
For Love transforms our Souls
into students of Divinity,
where we sit in the valley of Humility
and on the plain of Truth,
and rest on the mountain of Love.
And because all things are consonant with God,
we find God in all things.
We have become joy itself,
swimming in the sea of Joy.
As joyous fire and flame of God,
our hearts sing forth Love's praise:

Sanctus

Presider: Every attachment
deprives us of the freedom
to wait upon God
in the present moment.

Trapped by anxious minds and fearful hearts
we search for someone to blame.

We feel as if we have fallen from grace
and are lost from the Holy Truth
of life cradled in Love.

We become convinced
that we are set apart from Love,
   guilty,
      judged,
         and shamed into suffering Souls.
In desperation we condemn others
and seek release in the delusion of revenge.

Yet the sea of Joy washes upon us
with relentless tenderness,
bearing our lifeless Souls
across the Red Sea.
With our own wrath
drowned in Christ,
our Souls live through the purity
of the unity
of the will
of God
that encloses all creation.

With Christ,
the Loved one,
our hearts now know:
there is no one except Him,
no one loves except Him,
for not one is except Him,
and thus He alone loves completely.

Lover, Loved, Love:
life is a banquet
flowing from the heart of the Triune God.
The Lover has annihilated Jesus,
and the Loved alone remains
who invites all to the table
spread upon the sea of Love.

                Mind, heart, body,
                     broken open,
                          shattered,
                                no walls existing –
the shimmering face of the Lover
cradles our countenance and says:
Receive, eat.
This is my Body, I am for you.
Remember, you can be no less for me.

Freely, the Loved pours forth his life.
This Soul is free,
        supremely free,
                in the stock,
                        in all her branches
and all the fruits of her braches.
Nothing but sweet flowing wine remains
and the Soul says:
Drink this, all of you:
This is my life Blood
a joyous Covenant from which flows
forgiveness of sin.
Remember, you can be no less for me.

Through Love and with Love and in Love,
in the unity of Holy Love,
to God be honor, glory, and praise,
for ever and ever.

All: **AMEN.**

Presider: As our Savior Christ has taught us, we now pray,

All: **Our Father in heaven,**
hallowed be your name.
Your kingdom come.
Your will be done on earth and in heaven.
Give us today the bread of life.
Forgive us our sins
as we forgive those who sin against us.
Save us from the time of trial
and deliver us from evil.
For the kingdom, the power,
and the glory are yours,
now and for ever. Amen.

The Breaking of the Bread

Presider: We break this bread
to share in the Body of Christ.
Assembly: **We who are many are one body,
for we all share in the one bread.**
Presider: The Gifts of God for the People of God.
All are invited to God's table.

Post-Communion Prayer
Presider: Christ, our Loved, speaks to us:
"You have been at my table,
    and I have given you my feast,
And you are so very well taught,
    and you have savored my feast so fully,
And my wines from the full barrel,
    by which you are so filled,
That the bouquet alone makes you inebriated,
    and you will never be other."

inspired by Marguerite Porete

*The version of the Lord's Prayer is from
St. Gregory of Nyssa, San Francisco, CA*

END NOTES

[i] Hafiz, "Come Dance," *The Gift: Poems by Hafiz*, Translations by Daniel Ladinsky (New York: Compass, 1999), 270.

[ii] Hafiz, "You Better Start Kissing Me," *I Heard God Laughing: Renderings of Hafiz*, by Daniel Ladinsky (Oakland, CA: Mobius Press, 1996), 77.

[iii] Meister Eckhart, "Sermon Two: Creation: A Flowing Out But Remaining Within," in Matthew Fox, *Passion for Creation: The Earth-Honoring Spirituality of Meister Eckhart* (Rochester, Vermont: Inner Traditions, 2000), 66.

[iv] Catherine Keller, *Face of the Deep*, 221.

[v] Athanasius, *De Incarnatione* or *On the Incarnation* 54:3, PG 25:192B.

[vi] Margarete Porete, *Miroeur*, 98, Chap. 30.

[vii] Sebastian Brock, *The Luminous Eye: The Spiritual World Vision of Saint Ephrem the Syrian* (Kalamazoo, Michigan: Cistercian Publications, 1992), 154.

[viii] Irenaeus of Lyons, *Against* Heresies V.

[ix] Athanasius, *De Incarnatione* or *On the Incarnation* 54:3, PG 25:192B.

[x] *Dogmatic Poem* 10:5; PG 37:465. Quoted in Kilian McDonnell, *The Baptism of Jesus in the Jordan: The Trinitarian and Cosmic Order of Salvation* (Collegeville, Minnesota: The Liturgical Press, 1996), 129.

[xi] *Catechetical Oration* 25; PG 45:65, 68. Quoted in McDonnell, *The Baptism of Jesus in the Jordan,* 129.

[xii] Meister Eckhart, quoted in Bernard McGinn, *The Mystical Thought of Meister Eckhart: The Man From Whom God Hid Nothing* (New York: Herder and Herder, 2001), 161.

[xiii] Julian *Showings* (Long Text) 27:225 quoted in Nuth, *God's Lovers in an Age of Anxiety*, 117.

[xiv] Nicholas of Cusa, *De filiatione Dei,* I h 52, Bond, quoted in Nancy J. Hudson, *Becoming God: The Doctrine of Theosis in Nicholas of Cusa* (Washington, D.C.: The Catholic University of America Press, 2007), 167.

[xv] *Hymns on Faith* 73:1; CSCO 155:192 and *Hymns on Faith* 74:3-4; CSCO 155:194, quoted in McDonnell, *The Baptism of Jesus in the Jordan*, 122-124.

[xvi] All of which might be a description of how God is present with creation. Some scholars draw upon the ancient Jewish doctrine of the Shekinah, and think of the creation of the universe as involving a withdrawal of God to make space for creatures. God makes space for the emergence of a universe and for the evolution of life and then embraces it *within* the divinity. Contemporary scholar Elizabeth Johnson draws comparison here with the pregnant mother: "To be so structured that you have room inside yourself for another to dwell is quintessentially a female experience. Every human being has lived and moved and had their being inside a woman, for the better part of the year it took them to be knit together." Theologian Denis Edwards says he finds "this experience of a mother making space in the womb for another a wonderfully rich and evocative image for the divine generativity by which the universe is brought forth within God."

[xvii] 4.8-10 (Mary King, *Gospel of Mary of Magdala*, 14.)

[xviii] For a fuller explanation of the meaning of "integral" within an integral sacramental vision, see my book, *Holding Beauty in My Soul's Arms*.

[xix] Angelus Silesius, quoted by Catherine Keller, *Face of the Deep: A Theology of Becoming* (New York: Routledge, 2003), 216. For more, see *The Cherubinic Wanderer*.

[xx] J. Philip Newell, *Celtic Benediction* (Grand Rapids, MI: William B. Eerdmans Publishing Company, 2001), 20.

[xxi] Richard Rohr. Center for Action and Contemplation. http://www.cacradicalgrace.org/.

[xxii] "The first images of the crucified Christ on the cross appeared in the early fifth century. The first of these images appears on a carved wood panel from the doors of the Basilica of Santa Sabina. Jesus is shown with the two thieves. The three figures are standing on the ground with their arms outstretched, the elbows slightly bent. Nails are visible in the hands, but there is only the suggestion of crosses." Ronald Zawilla, "Cross and Crucifix in the Christian Assembly - Part II (The Early Christian Period: Christus Victor)," *Envision Church: Art, Architecture, Liturgy, and Spirituality in the Catholic Tradition* (October 30, 2007), http://www1.georgetown.edu/centers/liturgy/envisionchurch/40402.html.

[xxiii] Rita Nakashima Brock and Rebecca Ann Parker, *Saving Paradise: How Christianity Traded Love of This World for Crucifixion and Empire* (Boston: Beacon Press, 2008), 268-70.

[xxiv] *MM* XXI, 410, quoted in Nancy J. Hudson, *Becoming God: The Doctrine of Theosis in Nicholas of Cusa* (Washington, D.C.: The Catholic University of America Press, 2007), 21.

[xxv] Marcus J. Borg, *The Heart of Christianity: Rediscovering a Life of Faith* (New York: HarperCollins, 2004), 111.

BIBLIOGRAPHY

Abelard, Peter. "Exposition of the Epistle to the Romans." Thelma Megill-Cobbler, "A Feminist Rethinking of Punishment Imagery in Atonement." *Dialog* 35 [winter 1996].

Adams, William Seth. *Shaped by Images: One Who Presides.* Church Publishing: New York, 1995.

Aitken, Robert, and Steindl-Rast, Brother David. *The Ground We Share: Everyday Practice, Buddhist and Christian.* Shambhala: Boston, 1996.

Almaas, A.H. *Facets of Unity: The Enneagram of Holy Ideas.* Diamond Books: Berkeley, California, 1998.

Almaas, A.H. *The Inner Journey Home: Soul's Realization of the Unity of Reality.* Shambhala: Boston, 2004.

Almaas, A.H. *The Pearl Beyond Price: Integration of Personality into Being: An Object Relations Approach.* Diamond Books: Berkeley, California, 1988.

Almaas, A.H. *The Point of Existence: Transformations of Narcissism in Self-Realization.* Shambhala: Boston, 2001.

Armstrong, Karen. *Buddha.* A Lipper/Viking Book: New York, 2001.

Athanasius, *De Incarnatione* or *On the Incarnation* 54:3, PG 25:192B.

The Autobiography of St. Teresa of Avila. Translated by Kieran Kavanaugh and Otilio Rodriguez. New York: One Spirit, 1987.

Bailie, Gil. *Violence Unveiled: Humanity at the Crossroads.* Crossroad: New York, 1995.

Barnhart, Bruno. *The Future of Wisdom: Toward a Rebirth of Sapiential Christianity.* Continuum: New York, 2007.

Barnhart, Bruno. *Second Simplicity: The Inner Shape of Christianity.* Paulist Press: New York, 1999.

Bhagavad Gita. Translated by Stephen Mitchell. Three Rivers Press: New York, 2000.
Bielecki, Tessaa. *Teresa of Avila: Mystical Writings.* New York: Crossroad, 1994.

Bilinkoff, Jodi. *The Avila of Saint Teresa: Religious Reform in a Sixteenth-Century City*. Ithaca, New York: Cornell University Press, 1989.

Borg, Marcus. *The God We Never Knew: Beyond Dogmatic Faith to a More Authentic Contemporary Faith*. HarperCollins: New York, 1998.

Borg, Marcus. *Jesus: A New Vision: Spirit, Culture, and the Life of Discipleship*. HarperCollins: New York: 1991.

Borg, Marcus. *Meeting Jesus again for the First Time: The Historical Jesus and the Heart of Contemporary Faith*. HarperCollins: New York, 1995.

Borg, Marcus, and Crossan, John Dominic. *The Last Week: The Day-by-Day Account of Jesus's Final Week in Jerusalem*. HarperSanFrancisco: New York, 2006.

Bourgeault, Cynthia. *The Meaning of Mary Magdalene: Discovering the Woman at the Heart of Christianity*. Shambhala: Boston, 2010.

Bourgeault, Cynthia. *The Wisdom Jesus: Transforming Heart and Mind – A New Perspective on Christ and His Message*. Shambhala: Boston, 2008.

Bourgeault, Cynthia. *The Wisdom Way of Knowing* : *Reclaiming an Ancient Tradition to Awaken the Heart*. Jossey-Bass: San Francisco, 2003.

Bouyer, Louis. *Eucharist: Theology and Spirituality of the Eucharistic Prayer*. University of Notre Dame Press: Notre Dame, Indiana, 1968.

Bradley, Ritamary. *Julian's Way: A Practical Commentary on Julian of Norwich*. London: HarperCollins *Religious*, 1992.

Brock, Rita Nakashima, and Parker, Rebecca Ann. *Proverbs of Ashes: Violence, Redemptive Suffering, and the Search for What Saves Us*. Beacon Press: Boston, 2001.

Brock, Rita Nakashima, and Parker, Rebecca Ann. *Saving Paradise: How Christianity Traded Love of this World for Crucifixion and Empire*. Beacon Press: Boston, 2008.

Brock, Sebastian. *The Luminous Eye: The Spiritual World Vision of Saint Ephrem the Syrian*. Cistercian Publications: Kalamazoo, 1992.

Brock, Sebastian. *The Syriac Fathers on Prayer and the Spiritual Life*. Cistercian Publications: Kalamazoo, 1988.

Brown, Raymond. *The Birth of the Messiah: A Commentary on the Infancy Narratives in the Gospels of Matthew and Luke.* Doubleday: New York, 1993.

Brown, Raymond. *The Death of the Messiah, From Gethsemane to the Grave Volume 1: A Commentary on the Passion Narratives in the Four Gospels.* Doubleday: New York, 1994.

Chetwynd, Tom. *Zen and the Kingdom of Heaven.* Wisdom Publications: Boston, 2001.

Chilton, Bruce. *Rabbi Jesus: An Intimate Biography.* Doubleday: New York, 2000.

Chupungco, Anscar J. *Liturgical Inculturation: Sacramentals, Religiosity, and Catechesis.* The Liturgical Press: Collegeville, Minnesota, 1992.

Chupungco, Anscar J. *Liturgies of the Future.* Wipf & Stock Publishers: Eugene, Oregon, 2006.

Clement, Oliver. *The Roots of Christian Mysticism: Texts from the Patristic Era with Commentary.* New City Press: New York, 1993.

Corbin, Henry. *The Man of Light in Iranian Sufism.* Translated by Nancy Pearson. Omega Publications: New Lebanon, New York, 1994.

Crossan, John Dominic. *The Historical Jesus: The Life of a Mediterranean Jewish Peasant.* HarperSanFrancisco: New York, 1992.

Crossan, John Dominic. *Who Killed Jesus? Exposing the Roots of Anti-Semitism in the Gospel Story of the Death of Jesus.* HarperSanFrancisco: New York, 1995.

Crossan, John Dominic, and Reed, Jonathan L. *In Search of Paul: How Jesus's Apostle Opposed Rome's Empire with God's Kingdom.* HarperSanFrancisco: New York, 2004.

Cunningham, David S. *These Three Are One: The Practice of Trinitarian Theology.* Blackwell Publishers: Malden, Massachusetts, 1998.

Cusa, Nicholas. "On Learned Ignorance." *Nicholas Cusa: Selected Spiritual Writings.* Translated by H. Lawrence Bond. New York: Paulist Press, 1997.

Danielou, Jean. *From Glory to Glory: Texts from Gregory of Nyssa's Mystical Writings.* Translated and Edited by Herbert Musurillo, S.J. St. Vladimir's Seminary Press. Crestwood, New York, 1979.

Delicious Laughter: Rambunctious Teaching Stories from the Mathnawi. Versions by Coleman Barks. Athens, Georgia: Maypop, 1990.

Edwards, Denis. *Jesus the Wisdom of God: An Ecological Theology.* Wipf & Stock Publishers: Eugene, Oregon, 2005.

Ernst, Carl W. *The Shambhala Guide to Sufism.* Shambhala: Boston, 1997.

Essential Sufism. Edited by James Fadiman and Robert Frager. HarperSanFrancisco: New York, 1997.

Fabian, Richard. *The Scandalous Table.* Unpublished paper, 2010.

Finlan, Stephan. *Options on Atonement in Christian Thought.* Liturgical Press: Collegeville, Minnesota, 2007.

Finlan, Stephan. *Problems with Atonement.* Liturgical Press: Collegeville, Minnesota, 2005.

Fischer, Norman. *Opening to You: Zen-Inspired Translations of the Psalms.* Viking Compass: New York, 2002.

Fowler, James W. *Stages of Faith: The Psychology of Human Development and the Quest for Meaning.* HarperCollins: New York, 1981.

Girard, René. *Things Hidden Since the Foundation of the World.* Translated by Stephen Bann and Michael Metteer. Stanford University Press: Stanford, California, 1987.

Girard, René. *Violence and the Sacred.* Translated by Patrick Gregory. The Johns Hopkins University Press: Baltimore, 1977.

Graham, Dom Aelred. *Zen Catholicism.* Crossroad: New York, 1999.

Green, Deirdre. *Gold in the Crucible: Teresa of Avila and the Western Mystical Tradition.* Worcester: Element, 1989.

Gregory of Nyssa: The Life of Moses. Translated by Abraham J. Malherbe and Everett Ferguson. Paulist Press: New York, 1978.

Griffiths, Bede. *The Marriage of East & West.* Templegate Publishers: Springfield, Illinois, 1982.

Griffiss, James E. *The Anglican Vision.* Cowley Publications: New York, 1997.

Grimes, Ronald L. *Deeply into the Bone: Re-Inventing Rites of Passage*. University of California Press: Berkeley, 2002.

Hafiz. *The Gift: Poems By Hafiz The Great Sufi Master*. Translated by Daniel Ladinsky. Penguin Compass: New York, 1999.

Hafiz. *I Heard God Laughing: Renderings of Hafiz*. By Daniel Ladinsky. Mobius Press: Oakland, CA: Mobius Press, 1996.

Haight, Roger. *Jesus: Symbol of God*. Orbis Books: Maryknoll, New York, 2000.

Hanh, Thich Nhat. *Going Home: Jesus and Buddha as Brothers*. Riverhead Books: New York, 1999.

Harmless, S.J., William. *Desert Christians: An Introduction to the Literature of Early Monasticism*. Oxford University Press: Oxford, 2004.

Harmless, S.J., William. *Mystics*. Oxford University Press: Oxford, 2008.

Helminski, Kabir Edmund. *Living Presence: A Sufi Way to Mindfulness & the Essential Self*. G.P. Putnam's Sons: New York, 1992.

Hildegard of Bingen: Mystical Writings. Edited by Fiona Bowie and Oliver Davies. Translated by Robert Carver. New York: Crossroad, 1990.

Hildegard of Bingen: Scivias. Translated by Mother Columba Hart and Jane Bishop. New York: Paulist Press, 1990.

Hildegard of Bingen's Book of Divine Works. Edited by Matthew Fox. Santa Fe, New Mexico: Bear & Company, 1987.

Holeton, David R. Editor. *Growing in Newness of Life: Christian initiation in Anglicanism Today*. Anglican Book Centre: Toronto, 1993.

Holeton, David R. *Our Thanks and Praise: The Eucharist in Anglicanism Today*. Anglican Book Centre: Toronto, 1998.

Hudson, Nancy J. *Becoming God: The Doctrine of Theosis in Nicholas of Cusa*. The Catholic University of America Press: Washington, D.C., 2007.

Jesus and Buddha: The Parallel Sayings. Marcus Borg, Editor. Seastone: Berkeley, California, 1997.

Johnston, William. *Christian Zen*. Fordham University Press: New York, 1997.

Julian of Norwich: Showings. Translated by Edmund Colledge and James Walsh. Paulist Press: New York, 1978.

The Kabir Book: Forty-Four of the Ecstatic Poems of Kabir. Versions by Robert Bly. Boston: Beacon Press, 1977.

Kadloubovsky, E., and Palmer, G.E.H. *Writings from the Philokalia: On Prayer of the Heart*. Faber and Faber: London, 1992.

Keating, Thomas. *Intimacy with God*. Crossroad: New York, 2009.

Keating, Thomas. *Manifesting God*. Lantern Books: New York, 2005.

Kennedy, Robert E. *Zen Gifts to Christians*. Continuum: New York, 2000.

Kennedy, Robert E. *Zen Spirit, Christian Spirit: The Place of Zen in Christian Life*. Continuum: New York, 2002.

Kharlamov, Vladimir. *The Beauty of the Unity and the Harmony of the Whole: The Concept of Theosis in the Theology of Pseudo-Dionysius the Areopagite*. WIPF & Stock: Eugene, Oregon, 2009.

King, Karen L. *The Gospel of Mary of Magdala: Jesus and the First Woman Apostle*. Polebridge Press: Santa Rosa, California, 2003.

LaCugna, Catherine Mowry. *God For Us: The Trinity and Christian Life*. HarperSanFrancisco: New York, 1991.

Lathrop, Gordon. *Holy Ground: A Liturgical Cosmology*. Minneapolis, MN: Fortress Press, 2003.

Lathrop, Gordon W. *Holy Things: A Liturgical Theology*. Augsburg Fortress: Minneapolis, 1993.

Lathrop, Gordon W. *Holy People: A Liturgical Ecclesiology*. Augsburg Fortress: Minneapolis, 1999.

Leloup, Jean-Yves. *The Gospel of Mary Magdalene*. Translated by Joseph Rowe. Inner Traditions: Rochester, Vermont, 2002.

Lai, Whalen, and von Brück, Michael. *Christianity and Buddhism: A Multicultural History of Their Dialogue*. Translated by Phyllis Jestice. Orbis Books: Maryknoll, New York, 2001.

Levine, Amy-Jill. *The Misunderstood Jew: The Church and the Scandal of the Jewish Jesus*. HarperOne: New York, 2006.

Lings, Martin. *A Sufi Saint of the Twentieth Century: Shaikh Ahmad al-Alawi*. The Islamic Texts Society: Cambridge, 1993.

Love Poems from God: Twelve Sacred Voices from the East and West. Translated by Daniel Ladinsky. Penguin Compass: New York, 2002.

Maharshi, Ramana. *The Collected Works of Ramana Maharshi*. Edited by Arthur Osborne. Weiser Books: Boston: York Beach, Maine, 1972.

Maharshi, Ramana. *The Spiritual Teaching of Ramana Maharshi*. Shambhala: Boston, 1988.

Malina, Bruce, and Rohrbaugh, Richard L. *Social-Science Commentary on the Synoptic Gospels*. Fortress Press: Minneapolis, 1992.

McDonnell, Kilian. *The Baptism of Jesus in the Jordan: The Trinitarian and Cosmic Order of Salvation*. Michael Glazier Books: Collegeville, Minnesota, 1996.

McGinn, Bernard. *The Flowering of Mysticism. Volume III of The Presence of God: A History of Western Christian Mysticism*. Crossroad: New York, 1998.

McGinn, Bernard. *The Foundations of Mysticism. Volume 1 of The Presence of God: A History of Western Christian Mysticism*. Crossroad: New York, 2003.

McGinn, Bernard. *The Growth of Mysticism. Volume II of The Presence of God: A History of Western Christian Mysticism*. Crossroad: New York, 1999.

McGinn, Bernard. *The Harvest of Mysticism in Medieval Germany (1300-1500). Volume IV of The Presence of God: A History of Western Christian Mysticism*. Crossroad: New York, 2005.

McGinn, Bernard. *The Mystical Thought of Meister Eckhart: The Man From Whom God Hid Nothing*. Crossroad: New York, 2003.

Maitri, Sandra. *The Enneagram of Passions and Virtues: Finding the Way Home*. Tarcher/Putnam, 2005.

Maitri, Sandra. *The Spiritual Dimension of the Enneagram*. New York: Tarcher/Putnam, 2000.

Meier, John P. *A Marginal Jew: Rethinking the Historical Jesus. Volume I: The Roots of the Problem and the Person*. Doubleday: New York, 1991.

Meier, John P. *A Marginal Jew: Rethinking the Historical Jesus. Volume Two: Mentor, Message, and Miracles.* Doubleday: New York, 1994.

Meier, John P. *A Marginal Jew: Rethinking the Historical Jesus. Volume Three: Companions and Competitors.* Doubleday: New York, 2001.

Meister Eckhart: The Essential Sermons, Commentaries, Treatises, and Defense. Translated by Edmund Colledge, O.S.A. and Bernard McGinn. New York: Paulist Press, 1981.

Merton & Sufism: The Untold Story. Edited by Rob Baker and Gray Henry. Fons Vitae: Louisville, Kentucky, 1999.

Merton, Thomas. *Mystics & Zen Masters.* Farrar, Straus and Giroux: New York, 1961.

Meyers, Ruth A. *Continuing the Reformation: Re-Visioning Baptism in the Episcopal Church.* Church Publishing: New York, 1997.

Mitchell, Nathan D. *Eucharist as Sacrament of Initiation.* Chicago: Liturgy Training Publications, 1994.

Moltmann, Jürgen. *The Trinity and the Kingdom.* Fortress Press: Minneapolis, 1993.

Newell, J. Philip, *The Book of Creation: An Introduction to Celtic Spirituality.* New York: Paulist Press, 1999.

Newell, J. Philip. *Celtic Benediction: Day and Night Prayer.* Wm. B. Eerdmans Publishing Co: Grand Rapids, Michigan, 2000.

Newell, J. Philip. *Celtic Prayers from Iona.* Paulist Press: New York, 1997.

Newell, J. Philip. *Listening for the Heartbeat of God: A Celtic Spirituality.* Paulist Press: New York: 1997.

Nicholas of Cusa: Selected Spiritual Writings. Translated by H. Lawrence Bond. Paulist Press: New York, 1997.
Nuth, Joan M. *God's Lovers in an Age of Anxiety: The Medieval English Mystics.* Maryknoll, New York: Orbis Books, 2001.

Pagels, Elaine. *Adam, Eve, and the Serpent.* Vintage Books: New York, 1989.

Pagels, Elaine. *Beyond Belief: The Secret Gospel of Thomas.* Random House: New York, 2003.

Pagels, Elaine. *The Origin of Satan*. Random House: New York, 1995.

Palmer, G.E.H., Sherrard, Philip, and Ware, Kallistos. *Philokalia: The Eastern Christian Spiritual Texts. Selections Annotated & Explained*. Annotation by Allyne Smith. Skylight Paths Publishing: Woodstock, Vermont, 2006.

Palmer, G.E.H., Sherrard, Philip, and Ware, Kallistos. *The Philokalia: The Complete Text, Volume 1*. Faber and Faber: London, 1979.

Palmer, G.E.H., Sherrard, Philip, and Ware, Kallistos. *The Philokalia: The Complete Text, Volume 2*. Faber and Faber: London, 1981.

Palmer, G.E.H., Sherrard, Philip, and Ware, Kallistos. *The Philokalia: The Complete Text, Volume 3*. Faber and Faber: London, 1984.

Palmer, G.E.H., Sherrard, Philip, and Ware, Kallistos. *The Philokalia: The Complete Text, Volume 4*. Faber and Faber: London, 1995.

Peacocke, Arthur. *Paths from Science towards God: The End of All Our Exploring*. Oneworld: Oxford, 2001.

Peacocke, Arthur. *Theology for a Scientific Age: Being and Becoming – Natural, Divine, and Human*. Fortress Press: Minneapolis, 1993.

Ponticus, Evagrius. *The Praktikos & Chapters on Prayer*. Translated by John Etudes Bamberger. Cistercian Publications: Kalamazoo, Michigan, 1981.

Porete, Marguerite. *The Mirror of Simple Souls*. Translated by Ellen L. Babinsky. New York: Paulist Press, 1993.

Power, David N. *The Eucharistic Mystery: Revitalizing the Tradition*. Crossroad: New York, 1997.

Procter-Smith, Marjorie. *In Her Own Rite: Constructing Feminist Liturgical Tradition*. OSL Publications: Nitro, West Virginia, 2000.

Procter-Smith, Marjorie, and Walton, Janet R. Editors. *Women at Worship: Interpretations of North American Diversity*. Westminster/John Knox Press: Louisville, Kentucky, 1993.

Pseudo-Dionysius: The Complete Works. Translated by Colm Luibheid. Paulist Press: New York, 1987.

Rahner, Karl. *The Trinity*. Continuum: New York, 2001.

Ramshaw, Gail. *God beyond Gender: Feminist Christian God-Language.* Augsburg Fortress: Minneapolis, 1995.

Ricoeur, Paul. *The Symbolism of Evil.* Beacon Press: Boston, 1967.

Rohr, Richard, and Ebert, Andreas. *The Enneagram: A Christian Perspective.* Crossroad: New York, 2001.

Rohr, Richard. *Everything Belongs: The Gift of Contemplative Prayer.* Crossroad: New York, 1999.

Rumi, Jelaluddin. *Delicious Laughter: Rambunctious Teaching Stories from the Mathnawi of Jelaluddin Rumi.* Versions by Coleman Barks. Maypop: Athens, Georgia, 1990.

Rumi, Jelaluddin. *The Essential Rumi.* Translated by Coleman Barks. HarperSanFrancisco: New York, 1995.

Rumi, Jelaluddin. *Rumi: The Book of Love: Poems of Ecstasy and Longing.* HarperSanFrancisco: New York, 2003.

Rumi, Jelaluddin. *The Soul of Rumi: A New Collection of Ecstatic Poems.* Translated by Coleman Barks. HarperSanFrancisco: New York, 2001.

Schneiders, Sandra M. *The Revelatory Text: Interpreting the New Testament as Sacred Scripture.* The Liturgical Press: Collegeville, Minnesota, 1999.

Schüssler Fiorenza, Elizabeth. *In Memory of Her: A Feminist Theological Reconstruction of Christian Origins.* Crossroad: New York, 1990.

Sealsoltz, Kevin R. Editor. *Living Bread, Saving Cup.* Liturgical Press: Collegeville, Minnesota, 1987.

Shah, Idries. *Caravan Dreams.* The Octagon Press: London, 1968.

Shah, Idries. *The Commanding Self.* The Octagon Press: London, 1994.

Shah, Idries. *The Sufis.* Anchor Books: New York, 1971.

Shah, Idries. *World Tales: The Extraordinary Coincidence of Stories Told in All Times, In All Places.* The Octagon Press: London, 1991.

Sherrard, Philip. *Christianity: Lineaments of a Sacred Tradition.* Holy Cross Orthodox Press: Brookline, Massachusetts, 1998.

Shorter, Aylward. *Toward a Theology of Inculturation.* Wipf & Stock Publishers: Eugene, Oregon, 2006.

Siegel, M.D., Daniel J. *The Developing Mind: How Relationships and the Brain Interact to Shape Who We Are.* The Guilford Press: New York, 1999.

Skudlarek, William, Editor, *The Continuing Quest for God: Monastic Spirituality in Tradition and Transition.* The Liturgical Press: Collegeville, Minnesota, 1982.

Smith, Houston. *Forgotten Truth: The Common Vision of the World's Religion.* HarperCollins: New York, 1992.

Smith, Houston. *The Soul of Christianity: Restoring the Great Tradition.* HarperSanFrancisco: New York, 2005.

Smith, Houston. *The World's Religions: Our Great Wisdom Traditions.* HarperSanFrancisco: New York, 1991.

Stegemann, Ekkehard, and Stegemann, Wolfgang. *The Jesus Movement: A Social History of Its First Century.* Translated by O.C. Dean, Jr. Minneapolis: Fortress Press, 1995.

Steindl-Rast, Brother David. *Deeper than Words: Living The Apostles' Creed.* Image: New York, 2010.

The Syriac Fathers on Prayer and the Spiritual Life. Translated by Sebastian Brock. Cistercian Publications Inc: Kalamazoo, Michigan, 1987.

Teasdale, Wayne. *A Monk in the World: Cultivating a Spiritual Life.* New World Library: Novato, California, 2002.

Teasdale, Wayne. *The Mystic Heart: Discovering a Universal Spirituality in the World's Religions.* New World Library: Novato, California, 1999.

Teresa of Avila. *The Life of Saint Teresa of Avila by Herself.* Translated by J. M. Cohen. London: Penguin Books, 1957.

Thew Forrester, Kevin G. *Holding Beauty in My Soul's Arms. Awakening to At-One-Ment: Being Transformed in Christ. Volume I: Faith Explorations.* LeaderResources: Leeds, Massachusetts, 2011.

Thew Forrester, Kevin L. *I Have Called You Friends: An Invitation to Ministry.* Church Publishing: New York, 2003.

Underhill, Evelyn. *Mysticism: The Nature and Development of Spiritual Consciousness.* OneWorld: Oxford, 1999.

Underhill, Evelyn. *Practical Mysticism.* Dutton: New York, 1943

Ward, Benedicta, Translator. *The Sayings of the Desert Fathers.* Cistercian Publications: Kalamazoo, Michigan, 1975.

Weil, Louis. *A Theology of Worship.* Cowley Publications: New York, 2001.

White, L. Michael. *From Jesus to Christianity.* HarperSanFrancisco: New York, 2004.

Wilber, Ken. *A Brief History of Everything.* Revised Edition. Shambhala: Boston, 2000.

Wilber, Ken. *The Eye of the Spirit: An Integral Vision for a World Gone Slightly Mad.* Shambhala: Boston, 1998.
Wilber, Ken. *Integral Spirituality: A Startling New Role for Religion in the Modern and Postmodern World.* Integral Books: Boston, 2006.

Wilber, Ken. *No Boundary: Eastern and Western Approaches to Personal Growth.* Shambhala: Boston, 2001.

Wilber, Ken. *Sex, Ecology, Spirituality: The Spirit of Evolution.* Shambhala: Boston, 2000.

Wink, Walter. *Engaging the Powers: Discernment and Resistance in a World of Domination.* Fortress Press: Minneapolis, 1992.

Wink, Walter. *The Human Being: Jesus and the Enigma of the Son of the Man.* Fortress Press: Minneapolis, 2002.

Wink, Walter. *Naming the Powers*: The Language of Power in the New Testament. Fortress Press: Minneapolis, 1984.

Wink, Walter. *Unmasking the Powers: The Invisible Forces That Determine Human Existence.* Fortress Press: Minneapolis, 1986.

Winkler, Gabriele. "The Origins and Idiosyncrasies of the Earliest Form of Asceticism." *The Continuing Quest for God: Monastic Spirituality in Tradition and Transition.* William Skudlarek, O.S.B., General Editor. Collegeville, MN: The Liturgical Press, 1982.

Wren, Brian. *What Language Shall I Borrow: God-Talk in Worship: A Male Response to Feminist Theology*. Wipf & Stock: Eugene, Oregon, 1989.

Zizioulas, John D. *Being as Communion: Studies in Personhood and the Church*. St. Vladimir's Seminary Press: Yonkers, New York, 1997.

About the Author

Kevin G. Thew Forrester lives with his wife, Rïse, and their two children, Miriam and Liam, in Marquette, Michigan. He has served the Diocese of Northern Michigan for the past ten years, initially as the Diocesan Ministry Development Coordinator and more recently as the Ministry Developer and Rector with St. Paul's, Marquette and St. John's, Negaunee.

Before coming to Northern Michigan, Kevin and Rïse were Co-Missioners in Central Oregon, nurturing mutual ministry. Kevin also served as the Diocesan Ministry Development Coordinator. While working with St. Michael & All Angels of Portland, Oregon, and serving as the Vicar of Church of the Four Winds, in the mid-1990's, he collaborated with Sonja Miller in the Diocese of Oregon to create the diocesan task force, Ministry of All the Baptized.

Kevin is a past coordinator of Living Stones, as well as a founding member of The Ministry Developers Collaborative, and occasional lecturer at Episcopal Divinity School. Kevin is an editor of and contributor to *LifeCycles: Christian Transformation in Community*, and has travelled throughout the U.S., Canada, Wales, England, and Scotland, to lead workshops on baptismal life and ministry in the post-modern 21st century. He is a certified teacher of the Enneagram in the Narrative Tradition as well as a trainee of the Integral Institute. In 2004, Kevin received Zen Buddhist lay ordination, called *jukai*. He founded the Healing Arts Center at St. Paul's, which hosts Enneagram workshops, weekly meditation, and faith explorations in the spiritual practices of the major faith traditions.

Kevin received his M.A. in Systematic Theology and Ph.D. in Moral Theology from The Catholic University of America, where he was the first non-ordained Resident Minister of Campus Ministry. He engaged in post-doctoral studies at both The Church Divinity School of the Pacific where he received an M.T.S., focusing in the areas of liturgics and bioethics, as well as at Lucille Salter Packard Children's Hospital at Stanford for a 9-month Bioethics Residency.

He is the author of two previous books: *Leadership and Ministry Within a Community of Equals* (InterCultural Ministry Development, San Jose, CA) and *I Have Called You Friends* (Church Publishing).

Made in the USA
Lexington, KY
13 December 2019